Praise for *Awaken Every Day*

"Thubten Chodron's calm, confident, and inviting
voice will be an inspiration as well as a solace to
new and experienced practitioners."
—Sylvia Boorstein, author of *Happiness Is an Inside Job*

"A treasure chest of sound advice to start each day with
inspiration. A welcome addition to anyone's calendar."
—Alexander Berzin, author of studybuddhism.com

"Whether your goal is awakening or simply to have a happy,
healthy life, this pithy compendium of Buddhist wisdom is
an excellent guide. Perhaps no one is better than Venerable
Thubten Chodron at presenting this ancient wisdom in
clear ways that make it easy to understand and apply in the
everyday moments of our lives. Make this wonderful book
a part of your every day, and watch your life transform.
Highly recommended!"
—Russell Kolts, Eastern Washington University, author of
The Compassionate-Mind Guide to Managing Your Anger

ALSO BY THUBTEN CHODRON

AWAKEN
EVERY DAY

365 Buddhist Reflections
to Invite Mindfulness
and Joy

Thubten Chodron

SHAMBHALA
Boulder
2019

Shambhala Publications, Inc.
4720 Walnut Street
Boulder, Colorado 80301
www.shambhala.com

9 8 7 6 5 4 3 2 1

First Edition
Printed in the United States of America

♾ This edition is printed on acid-free paper that meets the
American National Standards Institute Z39.48 Standard.
♻ This book is printed on 30% postconsumer recycled paper.
For more information please visit www.shambhala.com.

Shambhala Publications is distributed worldwide by
Penguin Random House, Inc., and its subsidiaries.

Library of Congress Cataloging-in-Publication Data
Names: Thubten Chodron, 1950– author.
Title: Awaken every day: 365 Buddhist reflections to invite
mindfulness and joy/Thubten Chodron.
Description: First edition. | Boulder: Shambhala, 2019.
Identifiers: LCCN 2018042845 | ISBN 9781611807165 (pbk.: alk. paper)
Subjects: LCSH: Buddhist devotional calendars. | Buddhism—
Doctrines. | Buddhist meditations. | Spiritual life—Buddhism.
Classification: LCC BQ5580.T48 2019 | DDC 294.3/4432—dc23
LC record available at https://lccn.loc.gov/2018042845

CONTENTS

INTRODUCTION

We live in an era when the world has become even more unpredictable; we don't know what information we can trust, and our communities feel divided. People want to know how to maintain a positive attitude and not succumb to despair or cynicism. All living beings want happiness and not suffering, and we human beings in particular seek meaning in our lives. We want to understand life and contribute to the well-being of others. Being confused about what causes true happiness and what causes suffering, we often sabotage our own and others' well-being. But the inner wish to learn and do better remains.

In recent years, Sravasti Abbey has received a stream of requests to speak about how to cultivate a constructive, healthy, and realistic motivation given what is happening in the country and the world. Reading a short spiritual passage each day steers us in a positive direction. We learn how to bring mindfulness and joy into our lives and how to subdue anger and increase compassion. Such knowledge is invaluable.

The idea for this book arose fortuitously. A friend in Singapore asked me to write a passage for each day of the year that people could read to learn about the Dharma

—the Buddha's precious teachings—and be inspired to become the kind of person they want to be. *Awaken Every Day: 365 Buddhist Reflections to Invite Mindfulness and Joy* was born.

This book was written for Buddhists and non-Buddhists alike, for all of us who want to learn how to subdue our anger and unruly desires and increase our compassion and wisdom. So many of the Buddha's teachings consist of practical methods that people of all faiths, as well as those who follow secular ethics, can embrace. For the most part, these daily reflections do not follow any particular sequence, so feel free to dip into them as you please. You may want to make the passage you read the theme of your day, using this brief teaching to guide you as you go about your daily activities. Or you may want to return to a specific entry repeatedly because it speaks to your heart. You will find that sentences in italics indicate thoughts, and sentences in quotation marks indicate spoken words. All the topics mentioned in *Awaken Every Day* are expanded in my other books as well as on my website (https://thubtenchodron .org) and in the daily talks I and other monastics give at Sravasti Abbey, many of which can be found at www.you tube.com/user/sravastiabbey.

The Buddha spoke of awakening from the sleep of ignorance regarding how phenomena actually exist as being the lasting state of freedom, joy, and fulfillment that is our spiritual aim. Just as you awaken each day from a good night's sleep, may you, by reading this book, progress on the path to awakening from the ignorance and disturbing emotions that cloud the brilliance of your buddha-nature.

My utmost respect and gratitude goes to the buddhas, bodhisattvas, and spiritual mentors who teach and guide us beings who mean well but who, due to our ignorance, create the causes of suffering for ourselves and others.

My teachers—especially His Holiness the Dalai Lama, Tsenzhap Serkong Rinpoche, and Kyabje Zopa Rinpoche—have been kind in sharing the Dharma with me over many decades. My motivation and inspiration comes from them, and my hope is to pass some of that on to you.

I thank my friends at Sravasti Abbey for their help and support while working on this volume, especially Venerables Thubten Tsultrim, Thubten Damcho, and Thubten Lamsel.

All errors are my own.

Bhiksuni Thubten Chodron
Sravasti Abbey, Newport, Washington

*365 Buddhist Reflections
to Invite Mindfulness and Joy*

I

Another Day to Practice

Today we woke up, so the day started off well. We can rejoice that we have another day to learn and practice the Buddha's teachings (the Dharma), to cultivate a kind heart, and to let go of the misconceptions and disturbing emotions that cloud our minds. We don't know how long we'll live or when death will come, so we need to be fully present in life and make wise decisions. Let's generate the intention to take care in our thoughts, words, and deeds, since what we do today will have consequences for ourselves and others far into the future.

2

The Power of Motivation

⸻

Motivation is the key factor that determines the value and benefit of whatever we do. We can look good on the outside and appear to be doing the right thing, but our actions are not virtuous if our motivation is rotten.

Try to begin any activity by generating a motivation based on love, compassion, and altruism. Continually investigate why you're doing a certain thing and why you're saying the words you're uttering so that your good motivation remains constant.

Even if you don't spontaneously feel love and compassion in your heart, repeatedly bringing your mind back to a motivation of kindness has a profound impact. Over time, this creates the foundation for you to have genuine love, compassion, and altruism for all beings.

3

Three Daily Aspirations

Each morning, renew your motivation by making three strong aspirations:

Today, as much as possible, I won't harm anybody.

Today, as much as possible, I will be of benefit and service to others.

Today, I will hold in my mind the bodhicitta motivation to attain awakening for the benefit of all beings.

Setting these three motivations daily is a precious practice that influences your entire day. Try to hold them in your mind as you go about your daily activities. Doing so is a great aid to recognizing and letting go of negative thoughts and cultivating beneficial ones.

If you tend to forget to set your motivation when you wake up, place a Post-it note on your alarm clock, bathroom mirror, refrigerator, or wherever it might help you remember these three thoughts throughout the day.

4

What Is Dharma Practice?

Practicing the Dharma means transforming your mind, becoming the kind of person you want to be. This is a slow process because we have many old habits, such as telling ourselves, *I can't change. I'm just an angry, self-centered person. I'm hopeless.*

Such discouragement is actually a form of laziness because if we've given up on ourselves we won't practice. We must learn to recognize and stop these unbeneficial thoughts rather than believing them and following them. Instead of bowing down to our afflictions—our disturbing emotions and misconceptions—we must call them out as the thieves that steal our happiness. Chief among the afflictions are the "three poisons:" ignorance, attachment, and animosity. Blinded by the ignorance that misapprehends how things actually exist, we generate attachment that clings to whatever appears attractive to us. When our desires are frustrated, animosity—which wants to destroy or get away from whatever we deem undesirable or unpleasant—arises. When afflictions manifest, we must invoke our wisdom and compassion to counteract them, restoring balance and peace to our minds.

Real Dharma practice involves confronting our afflictions when they arise and applying the antidotes—the "medicine" the Buddha offered to quell our suffering. We must be patient with ourselves as we do this inner transformative work. We can't accomplish it all at once.

5

More Than Just This Life

An ordinary worldview considers just this life. We think, *Here I am, an individual "me."* We don't think of ourselves as being part of a continuum or as being influenced by causes and conditions. Such a worldview makes it difficult to practice the Dharma because our motivations are focused only on the happiness of this life.

The Buddhist worldview includes rebirth and karma. Our mindstreams will continue beyond this life, extending to future lives, and our present actions (our karma) have an ethical dimension that will influence our future lives and our experiences in those lives. This view gives us a much broader perspective on life, one that changes how we see ourselves and the purpose of our lives.

Having this expansive outlook is important in developing the right motivation and perspective for practice. It's helpful to spend time contemplating the four truths, the foundation of the Buddha's teachings, because they give us an accurate understanding of how we fit into the continuum of life in the universe. These four truths concern our present unsatisfactory situation; its causes, which abide in our minds; the possibility of freedom from this cycle; and the path leading to liberation.

6

A Healthy Mind

~

When I look at what I think about all day long and ask myself, *Are these the thoughts I want to have when I'm dying? Are these the imprints I want to put in my mindstream and take into my future lives?* the answer is usually no.

We spend so much time on thoughts like *Does that person like me? Do I fit in? What are they saying about me?* Our obsession with reputation and others' opinions of us is by and large useless. What others think doesn't change who we are. We must learn to assess ourselves realistically—acknowledging our faults, purifying our misdeeds, and rejoicing in our talents and what we do well.

Learning the Buddha's teachings helps us to think in a healthy and realistic manner and avoid unrealistic thoughts that only make us anxious and fearful. Remembering impermanence and death helps us cut self-indulgence and guilt and helps us cultivate virtuous mental states that can transform our words and actions.

7

The Patient, the Doctor, the Nurses, and the Medicine

~

We're like a patient; our disease is cyclic existence—taking one rebirth after another under the influence of ignorance and karma. During each lifetime we suffer from not getting what we want, encountering difficulties, and separating from the people and possessions we treasure.

We go to the Buddha, who is the doctor that diagnoses our disease and identifies its causes. He says: "You're suffering from the first noble truth, true *duḥkha* (unsatisfactory circumstances). You have a body that you can't always control; you are born, age, fall sick, and die without choice. The spiritual virus that is causing your condition is true origins: chiefly ignorance, which gives rise to afflictions such as attachment, animosity, and confusion. You need to take the medicine, the true path—the wisdom realizing the nature of reality. Specifically, the medicine is the wisdom realizing emptiness. This will lead you to a state of perfect health—the third truth, true cessation—nirvana, which is the cessation of all duhkha and its causes."

After receiving the doctor's prescription, we must obtain the medicine and take it. If we leave it on the nightstand, we won't heal. Sometimes we forget how to take the medicine. The Sangha—the people who have directly realized the nature of reality—are like nurses who remind us to take the medicine and clarify how to take it. By taking the Dharma medicine and following the Buddha's instructions with the help of the Sangha, we will have vibrant health and be able to smile at the world no matter what happens.

8

Honey on a Razor Blade

~~~~~~

Attachment is like honey on a razor blade. The honey tastes so sweet as we're licking it off the blade, but simultaneously we're hurting ourselves.

This is the deceptive quality of clinging to the things of this life, thinking that they will bring us happiness. Generally, there is a pleasurable feeling in the mind when attachment is present. We're so addicted to this low-grade, fleeting happiness that we opt for it without realizing its dangers: It is a set-up for misery because it is fleeting and brings us a new set of problems. For example, as soon as we have a new car, we become susceptible to "car hell" when the car breaks down or gets damaged. Attachment to the fleeting happiness of possessions, status, and so forth blinds us to the fulfillment of awakening and the bliss of liberation, which are stable forms of joy and satisfaction. Instead, we keep licking the honey off the razor blade.

It's not enough to remember the disadvantages of attachment intellectually. We need to examine our life and find many examples of how it deceives us and brings us suffering in the here and now, as well as impedes our chance for liberation.

9

Our Actions Bring Effects

Karma refers to our intentional physical, verbal, and mental actions—what we do, say, and think. Our actions leave "seeds" on our mindstream, invisible potentials that can bring results in terms of what we experience in this and future lives—our habitual thoughts and behaviors and the environment and circumstances of our life. Our actions have an ethical dimension: happiness comes from virtue, unhappiness from nonvirtue. The Buddha doesn't reward or punish us—he is not a Creator God. What we experience comes from our own minds, so we are responsible for the causes we create. This being so, let's consider well our choices and decisions.

10

Natural Love and Compassion

When we meditate deeply and repeatedly on the kindness of others, we understand that we've been the recipient of tremendous kindness throughout our lives. We begin to see kindness all around us and, in response, the wish to reciprocate and pay it forward naturally arises.

The happiness we experience when we express our love and kindness to others is qualitatively different from that which arises from following a self-centered attitude. Love, which wants others to have happiness and its causes, and compassion, which seeks to free others from suffering and its causes, bring more inner peace than winning the lottery.

II

Being Kind to Yourself

In worldly ways, being kind to yourself is often confused with being self-indulgent.

In Buddhism, kindness means doing what's best for yourself in the long run, which entails practicing the Buddhist path. The basis of the path is taking refuge, making the thoughtful decision to entrust our spiritual guidance to the Three Jewels—the Buddha, the Dharma, and the Sangha. We also decide to keep the five precepts: refraining from killing, from taking what is not given, from unwise and unkind sexual behavior, from lying, and from taking intoxicants. These are the ways we take care of ourselves and protect ourselves from suffering. Harming our enemies doesn't protect us; it encourages them to retaliate and inflict more harm on us. In addition, by causing harm to others we plant the seeds of destructive karma on our mindstream, and these seeds will ripen in future lives as conditions that will bring suffering.

On the other hand, the Buddha, the Dharma, and the Sangha provide a path that leads us out of the unsatisfactory conditions of cyclic existence. By practicing this path, we cast off the shackles that keep us imprisoned, and we awaken to the peace and joy that is nirvana.

Just look, have you ever seen an unhappy Buddha?

12

The Source of Happiness and Misery

Our minds are the source of both happiness and misery. This happens in two ways. First, our moods and attitudes color our experiences here and now. An angry mind sees negativities and is unhappy. A relaxed mind is open, tolerant, and curious. Whether our mind is happy or miserable in a given situation depends heavily on our outlook.

Second, our actions are motivated by our mental states, which influence the situations we will encounter in the future and how we will experience them. While constructive actions that are motivated by kindness, compassion, generosity, and so forth bring peace and contentment in this life and a good rebirth, destructive actions not only harm ourselves and others now, they bring us painful results in future lives.

Understanding the way the mind creates happiness and suffering, we see that we have the ability to transform our circumstances and experiences by changing our thoughts and emotions.

13

Benefiting Ourselves and Others

We practice the Dharma not because we want to be great yogis and yoginis and famous spiritual practitioners, nor do we do it just for our own liberation. We cultivate the motivation to free ourselves from cyclic existence and attain full buddhahood so that we can benefit others now and lead them on the path to freedom and full awakening in the future. This vast approach of working for the benefit of self *and* others also increases our short-term happiness.

On the other hand, if we act with a motivation that disregards others and seeks only our own benefit, we're working against our long-term goal of awakening. Happiness is not a fixed pie, whereby if someone else has it, we don't. Benefiting ourselves and benefiting others comes to the same point. If we help others, we live around happy people, which makes our lives more pleasant too. Keep this in mind as you go about your daily activities and examine whether or not this is true in your experience.

14

Growing Faith

As someone new to Buddhism, I wondered, *How do I know the Buddha exists? Many people say so, but how do I really know?*

The growth of my faith depended very much on having a personal taste of the Buddha's teachings. As I studied, I began to understand the basic layout of the path—what the mind is, how it is obscured by mental afflictions such as attachment, anger, and confusion, and how these defilements can be removed. When I practiced the antidotes to the afflictions, there was a positive effect on my mind. For example, instead of ruminating on all the reasons I didn't like someone, which only increased my anger and resentment, I practiced seeing them as someone who just wanted to have happiness and was confused about how to create its causes. As a result, I didn't get angry as much, and depression no longer plagued me.

That gave me faith that the Buddhist path works and led me to think that if I practiced this path, maybe it is possible for deeper changes to occur in my mind. That gave me more confidence that there are indeed holy beings and a path to attain their state.

15

The Power of the Dharma

When we don't understand the power of the Dharma—the one true thing we can rely on—we take refuge in other human beings to guide, protect, and shelter us from the travails of life. However, others are also caught up in cyclic existence and are just as confused as we are. They lack the ability to protect us from suffering, just as we cannot protect them from suffering. We may have compassion for others, but we cannot make them change and live a healthier lifestyle.

We've all had the experience of being in a wonderful situation—lying on a beach, talking to our friends, eating good food, listening to music we like—and still being miserable because our minds are filled with anger, resentment, jealousy, and dissatisfaction. Happiness has more to do with the state of our mind than with external circumstances. We may pray to the Buddha to change our external situation without realizing that what we really need to change is our own physical, verbal, and mental actions.

The path to happiness is not about changing the outside world; it's about applying the Dharma in order to change our outlook and emotions.

16

How the Buddha Helps Us

The Buddha is not an omnipotent God to whom we pray to bring us the good situations, love, and success we crave. The Buddha teaches us the methods to counteract the mental afflictions that are the source of our turmoil. He instructs us in how to engage in virtuous actions that are the source of happiness and how to eliminate nonvirtuous actions that are the cause of pain. This gives us the power to change our experience by putting the teachings into practice. The Buddha cannot pull switches to change the way we think; he cannot modify the synapses in our brain or create a pill that brings instant awakening. If that were possible, the Buddha would have done it already. The chief way the Buddha benefits us is through teaching us; our job is to put the teachings into practice.

17

My Religion Is Kindness

~

His Holiness the Dalai Lama says, "My religion is kindness." That hits home, doesn't it? No matter what religion, if any, you follow, or what social policies you advocate, kindness connects all of us. We are each born into kindness. We know this because we are alive now. If others didn't take care of us when we were little, we would have died a long time ago.

When understood correctly, religion and theology tells us that kindness is in our own best interests. Unfortunately though, sometimes we use religion to fight and destroy our own and others' well-being. We quarrel over theology and philosophy and kill one another in the name of God. But true spirituality isn't about ideas, it's about action. All of us appreciate kindness, so let's act in ways that give kindness to others.

18

Cleaning Out Our Garbage

If we review our life—or even just the past year—with honesty, we'll notice the times when the garbage in our minds has led us to make bad decisions. Alarmed, we may scream, "Woe is me! This is too much to handle!" and then go to the bar, shopping mall, casino, refrigerator, or movies. This attitude and the actions it inspires get us nowhere.

Our old habits of low self-esteem, self-criticism, and defeatism are some of the garbage to abandon. Instead of wallowing in such unrealistic thoughts, we must leave the rubbish behind. Whenever you find garbage thoughts and feelings in your mind, use that to strengthen your refuge in the Three Jewels—the Buddha, the Dharma, and the Sangha—and renew your determination to change. Remember, to clean a room, we must first see the dirt. Similarly, to clean your mind, you must first recognize the trash there. So rejoice when you see it because now you can clean it up.

19

Change Is Possible

It is possible to liberate our minds from garbage because those wrong views and disturbing emotions are not embedded in the nature of our minds. They are like storm clouds that temporarily obscure the wide-open sky but are not part of the sky. Because afflictions are based on ignorance, which sees things in a way opposite to how they actually exist, when we realize how things do exist, ignorance is banished. When ignorance, the root of cyclic existence, ceases, all the afflictions that come with it shrivel and die. The pure nature of the mind remains.

20

Good Qualities Can Be Cultivated Limitlessly

Good qualities such as love, compassion, forgiveness, generosity, fortitude, ethical conduct, and so on can be consciously cultivated, and disturbing emotions can be eradicated through learning and practicing the correct methods to do so. Unlike a high jumper who must cover the same distance jumped the previous day plus some in order to improve, if we practice consistently we can build directly on the good qualities cultivated the previous day without needing to tread ground already covered.

21

Sweet Constraints

—

Whatever we do in life, constraints help it to go well. Otherwise there's danger that our mental afflictions of anger, clinging, and confusion will take over and we will stop caring if we harm someone, even ourselves. To prevent this, we voluntarily undertake "sweet constraints" because we've understood their purpose and the reason for them. They nurture the best in us and help us grow.

In Buddhism, the sweet constraints are the ethical precepts, which are never imposed on us from outside. We voluntarily adopt them because they guide the actions of our body, speech, and mind toward virtue and prevent us from doing things we don't want to do. The precepts are a form of real protection that helps us grow in a positive direction and live harmoniously with others.

22

Refuge Gives Us Hope

Taking refuge daily in the Three Jewels—the Buddha, the Dharma, and the Sangha—helps us overcome feelings of hopelessness, helplessness, and meaninglessness. Turning to the Three Jewels for guidance by studying and practicing the Dharma teachings gives us clarity and confidence about what we're doing and where we're heading in life.

Refuge in the Dharma, especially, reminds us that ignorance, afflictions, and karma *can* be counteracted. There *is* a path to train our minds to eradicate the afflictions, and there *is* a way to overcome our self-centeredness and work wholeheartedly for the benefit of all living beings.

This worldview inspires us to practice the path to attain liberation and awakening, which gives our lives great meaning and purpose.

23

What Can We Rely On?

We want to find something that will bring us reliable happiness, but mostly we go from the frying pan into the fire.

Taking refuge is not a new activity. We do it throughout the day. When we're bored, we take refuge in our devices. When we're lonely, we take refuge in person A. But when we realize that person isn't everything we painted them to be, we become dissatisfied and take refuge in person B. But they aren't all we want either. It's impossible to satisfy our self-centered minds.

It's time to stop running around and instead find trustworthy spiritual guides and then follow the path they teach. The Buddha, the Dharma, and the Sangha are those guides. May we be fortunate enough to meet them, understand them, and follow their guidance.

24

What Is Important When We Die?

We may have wealth, power, status, a great career, and fame. Other people may look at us and wish they had our life. But are we truly happy inside? When the time of death arrives, will we have regrets? I've never heard of anyone regretting that they didn't work more overtime.

To distance ourselves from unsatisfactory situations in cyclic existence, we reach for entertainment, food, sports—anything to distract us from looking inside and learning to become friends with ourselves. At the time of death, will we regret that we didn't engage in any of those worldly activities more than we did? Will we say, "I wish I'd seen more movies, read more novels, or watched more ballgames"? Or will we say, "I wish I'd been kinder to other people and to animals, I wish I'd learned more about the true nature of existence, I wish I'd connected with others and helped them more"?

25

Developing Self-Confidence

~~~~~~

We've been taught to compare ourselves with others and to compete with them to be the best. But does being the best in a competition make us a worthwhile person? Does it mollify our lack of self-confidence? Or does being the best create more stress because we worry we won't be able to maintain that place in the future?

Instead of basing our self-respect on what other people think of us and how we rank among others, let's use the fact that we have the buddha-nature—the potential to become fully awakened buddhas—as the basis of our self-confidence. The buddha-nature is an inalienable part of our minds that can never disappear. Each of us has unique talents and abilities to offer the world, so let's tap into those and develop them and abandon comparing ourselves to others.

26

Concern with What Others Think of Us

Sometimes our minds worry about what others think of us. *Do they like me? Do I have a good reputation? Do they respect me?* Yet, what is a reputation? It is other people's thoughts. It's only thoughts, nothing substantial. We can't control others' thoughts, and believe it or not, usually people spend more time thinking about themselves than mulling over what they think about us. In addition, their thoughts about us change and vary. One person criticizes us for doing a certain action, while another person praises us for doing the same thing. If we base our self-esteem on others' opinions, we'll get very confused.

It's best to focus on improving the quality of our motivation so that we act with honesty and kindness. Then we'll feel good about ourselves and won't worry so much about what others think about us.

27

Overcoming Fear of Criticism

How often do we hear innocuous statements as criticism?

Someone asks you for a glass of water and you think, *Oh, I'm such a bad person—I should have given them water before they had to ask for it. What's wrong with me? I can't do anything right . . .*

This habit of imputing criticism where there is none can become an obstacle to our growth. We're afraid to even move our little toe because we might do it wrong.

It's worth paying attention to how much we put limits on ourselves out of fear of criticism. And when people do point out actual mistakes we made, instead of hearing criticism, let's use it as an opportunity to grow.

28

Internal Housekeeping

Our mind is like a yo-yo. When we're near someone or something we like, we feel happy and become attached to the pleasant feeling. When we encounter someone or something we deem unpleasant, we become unhappy and angry. If a situation or person doesn't affect us one way or another, we are apathetic and ignore it. We go up and down like a yo-yo many times each day in reaction to the people and situations we encounter. These three—attachment, anger, and ignorance—pretty much run our lives. This is our situation in cyclic existence.

The solution is to address our internal landscape—our thoughts and judgments. Instead of looking at people and events from the perspective of "does this please me?" let's see people more realistically. Everyone wants happiness and not suffering, everyone has been kind to us in one lifetime or another, so let's wish them well. Instead of getting down because it's raining and we wanted to be outdoors today, let's think of an indoor activity we'd like to do and rejoice that the weather gives us an opportunity to do that today.

29

Thinking for Ourselves

As children we had many experiences and heard many words that conditioned us. We didn't have a lot of wisdom at that age and couldn't discern what is true from what isn't, and so we usually just believed everything. On that basis we developed certain habitual views, biases, ideas, and emotional reactions. Some of these are true and serve us well. However, some are not true and keep us bound in negative emotions and behaviors. Now, as adults, we can look back on the conditioning we received as youngsters and decide with wisdom what to keep and what to discard. We may need to exert energy to recondition our minds to see things and respond to them more realistically and with a beneficial intention, but when we do we'll shed layers of mental dirt, and in this way we can freshly approach life.

30

A Dharma View of Death

~~~~~~

Most people fear death because they must separate from all that is familiar and loved—possessions, dear ones, and the body itself. This panicky fear of death makes dying tumultuous. In Buddhism we cultivate a wise concern regarding death. Because we know that one day we'll separate from all that is loved and valuable in this life and that only the seeds of our actions and our mental habits will continue to the next life, we want to make this life meaningful. To do so, we ask ourselves what is and is not important in life, and set our priorities accordingly. The Dharma practice that leads to inner transformation becomes a priority, and we are able to make clean, clear decisions in life, leaving confusion and doubts behind.

31

Transcending Death, Going to the Deathless

All of us beings bound in cyclic existence die again and again. Witnessing the reality of death propelled Prince Siddhartha to leave his worldly palace in search of the truth. As a result of his search, he became a fully awakened one.

Death is a reality of life under the influence of ignorance, afflictions, and karma. Recognizing this, we develop the strong intention to free ourselves from the causes of cyclic existence and gain nirvana, the deathless state, a state beyond death and rebirth.

Making Life Meaningful

We spend a lot of time thinking about the future, often making ourselves miserable in the present. Someone once wrote to me saying that she was afraid because she was ill and feared dying. Her fear was based on projecting events that hadn't happened yet and creating scenarios that didn't exist.

Similarly, we look into the future and anticipate that something's going to bring us happiness. We get excited even though nothing has actually happened. The excitement stirs up our minds and prevents us from connecting with people in the present.

The future hasn't happened yet. Although you may make plans in order to have some idea of what will happen, don't hold on to them too tightly. Come back to the present and what you can do now to make life meaningful.

33

Are You Angry?

My friend insulted me, and feeling sorry for myself I leave and go sulk. When my friend comes after me and says, "Are you angry? Are you upset?" I turn away and with a scowl, saying, "No! I'm not angry, mind your own business!" My friend leaves. At that moment what I really want is to connect with that person, yet hurt and angry, I push them away. My behavior brings the opposite of what I really want.

Sadly, when we're locked in anger, our words and actions often prevent communication with those we value most. Yet we're too proud to drop our hurt and express our love.

Has this ever happened to you?

34

Watering Seeds

When we associate with people who live ethically and value spiritual life, they nurture that part of us. Our mindstream contains the seeds of many tendencies, and depending on the environment we put ourselves in and who we befriend, certain seeds will grow and not others. Dharma friends nurture the Dharma seeds in our minds; lazy friends water our lazy seeds; resentful friends feed our resentment.

Which seeds do we want to grow and flower? According to what the answer is, we should cultivate those kinds of friends.

35

Our Enemies Suffer Too

—

Usually, when we think about people we put in the enemy category—those who have harmed us, who threaten us, whom we fear—we focus on our own suffering and how they've caused it. The Buddha suggests that we consider their suffering and change the focus from us to them. Instead of holding the idea, "They made me suffer," try stepping outside of yourself and look at their situation. When you focus on the fact that just like you, they too are bound by afflictions and karma in the net of cyclic existence, compassion for them will arise. When the wish for them to be free of suffering grows, your mind softens and your anger will dissipate.

36

Which Mind Are You?

We're familiar with the dictum "I think, therefore I am." We strongly feel that we are our mind, that our mind makes us the person we are. Even Buddhist scriptures say the mind is what goes from lifetime to lifetime.

We must look more closely. Are we really our mind? Within one day we have so many different mental states— happy, sad, contemplative, extroverted, introverted. If we are our mind, which mind are we? The awake mind, the sleeping mind, the dreaming mind? Are we the happy mind, the alert mind, the wisdom mind, the miserable mind, the spaced-out mind, the angry mind?

Search through all these different states of mind and see if you can find one that is you.

Maybe you aren't any of them.

Maybe you depend on all these different mental states and aren't any one of them.

37

Comfortable in Cyclic Existence

We may have heard many Dharma teachings, especially those about the disadvantages of cyclic existence, but when we think of our experience in cyclic existence it doesn't seem so bad. "Okay, I'm in cyclic existence, but as long as I'm relatively comfortable and people like me, a little bit of suffering is okay. This is not an unbearable prison; I have lots of freedom—I can say anything I want, do anything I want, have anything I want. Sometimes there are problems, but they're all other people's fault, and since there's nothing much I can do, I'll just enjoy myself. I'll live day to day, try to avoid suffering and have happiness, say a few mantras, and that's good enough."

Thinking like this resembles a person on death row who thinks prison is pretty spiffy. *I have a bed, three meals, and a TV. Sure, prison is a dangerous place, but I'll ignore that and enjoy the concrete walls topped with razor wire that sparkles in the sunlight.*

38

The Drawbacks of Cyclic Existence

The drawbacks of cyclic existence are three:

The first is outright physical or mental pain that nobody—not even animals and insects—likes and everybody wants to get rid of.

Second is the unsatisfactoriness of change. We experience pleasure, but neither the pleasure nor the object that seems to cause it lasts very long. In addition, if we repeatedly do the pleasurable activity, it becomes painful. Being with our dear ones alleviates loneliness, but if we are with them 24/7 with no break, we want to be alone. If the happiness were real happiness, the more we had contact with the person or object, the more pleasure we'd experience, but that's not the case. After eating a lot of food we enjoy, our stomach hurts. Nothing in cyclic existence can bring us lasting happiness.

Third, our bodies and minds are under the influence of ignorance, afflictions, and polluted karma. Being in this state means that even when we're not experiencing gross pain, we're always on the edge of a cliff. Any small change in our circumstances and happiness instantly disappears, replaced by suffering.

Isn't it time for us to think of liberation?

39

A Vivid Life

If we meditate on death and feel overwhelmed by feelings of loss and grief, we're coming to the wrong conclusion. Such feelings are based on attachment to our loved ones, our body, and our identity, and on the misunderstanding that holds transient things to be stable and enduring.

Instead of succumbing to fear, cultivate a Dharma perspective on death. Contemplating our mortality brings into vivid relief our incredible opportunity to practice the Dharma in this very lifetime. Given how short it is, make good use of your life and don't waste it on frivolous activities. Don't live on automatic, but instead create the causes for liberation and awakening.

40

Listening to the Wise

~

Buddhist practitioners and worldly people have very different priorities in life. Although we've heard many Dharma teachings, most of the time we're worldly people and wannabe practitioners. The worldly part tugs at us. It's hard to let that go and see that there's really no lasting happiness in cyclic existence.

When wise people like our spiritual mentors point out our faults, we need to pay attention—not out of attachment to our reputation, but because they're acting with compassion and have the wisdom that will benefit us.

41

Our Only Protection in Life

Some people are born into horrible circumstances but have comfortable lives when they're old. Others start out with wonderful lives but as they age, destructive karma ripens, and they experience great pain. Think about the aristocracy in China who were imprisoned and tortured during the Cultural Revolution. They didn't see that coming.

Our circumstances depend on multiple and complex causes and conditions, most of which we can't control. The time when we had some control was when we created the karma. Now, the only real protection we have in life is the Three Jewels, especially the Dharma Jewel. If we listen to the teachings, reflect and meditate on them, and integrate them in our minds, we will stop creating destructive karma that will ripen as future suffering. In addition, when previously created karma ripens as present suffering, we'll be able to transform those bad circumstances into the path to awakening. For example, we'll see them as opportunities to generate compassion for people whom we find disagreeable and fortitude that accepts illness without anger or despair.

42

No Time to Practice

It can be revealing to make a list of the things we typically ruminate over—likes and dislikes, fears and hopes, plans and regrets—and keep track of how much time we spend thinking about them. Then when we think, *I don't have any time to practice the Dharma*, we can see what we actually did with our time.

43

Keeping the Dharma in Our Hearts

A woman told me about a difficult situation she had for a few years. In hindsight, she realized that she had such a rough time because she had neglected to practice the Buddha's teachings. She thought that just because she had learned the Dharma it would always be in her heart. She believed that she would remember how to apply the teachings to her life whenever difficulties arose, even if she wasn't regularly practicing those teachings. After much suffering, she realized how foolish it was to think the Dharma would be there for her when she hadn't been there for it.

It's up to us to keep the Dharma in our hearts, to consistently remember the Buddhist worldview and the antidotes to the afflictions that the Buddha taught. If we consistently cultivate a Dharma perspective on life, the Dharma will always be there for us. We'll be able to easily recall the teachings when we need them.

44

The Core of Our Practice

~

Cultivating a proper motivation is the core of our practice. The long-term motivation to attain full awakening in order to benefit sentient beings most effectively will sustain us through the ups and downs of life. Why? Because we won't be seeking short-term benefit for ourselves.

The motivation to have peak experiences so we can brag about them to others or to become a Dharma teacher so we'll be famous and receive offerings won't sustain us in the long run. Such motivations contaminate our practice with attachment to worldly gain and fame, as in "I'm practicing so that I can make being a Dharma teacher my career."

Dharma is not a career. Dharma is our life.

45

Grief

Grief is adjusting to a change that we didn't want. We expected our life to unfold one way, and either the causes for that were absent or an unexpected event occurred.

Our grief is not for the past; the past is over. It is also not for the present, which is happening this instant. We're grieving for an idea that we held about the future that will not come to be. We're grieving for a future—something that hasn't happened yet—that now won't happen. Strange, isn't it?

When you lose a dear one, try rejoicing that the person was in your life for as long as they were. Rejoice at what you shared, and then take that joy and share it with others.

46

Big View

~

We aren't just the body and identity that we have now. There's a continuity of consciousness that's been going on without beginning and will continue infinitely without end. Buddhism says there's no soul or permanent self, an "I" that goes from one life to the next, although the actions done in previous lives—our karma—influences what we experience in this and future lives.

The more we can hold this big view of the continuity of our consciousness, the more our wrong views and grasping will diminish and the more attentive and relaxed our mind will become. We'll appreciate the functioning of cause and effect even though we are not inherently existent people who are independent of causes and conditions.

Try to hold this big view in your mind throughout the day, remembering that who you think you are is a hallucination created by the mind. There's not much sense in being attached to the notion of an "I" that is the center of the universe when such an "I" doesn't exist. Instead, open to this ever-flowing interconnectedness.

47

Karmic Bubbles

From the viewpoint of multiple lives, the person we are now—a person who exists by being merely designated in dependence on the present mind and body—is a karmic bubble that is continuously changing. We are a product of the interplay of innumerable actions we did in previous lives. Who we are right now is conditioned by an incredible complexity of causes. We're not solid, concrete personalities or discreet entities, but ever-changing phenomena that have no self-enclosed, individual essence.

Since we don't have an unchanging essence, but instead are dependent on causes and conditions, we can change. We can progress along the path and become fully awakened buddhas simply by changing our conditioning. This gives us a vision of who we can become and hope for the future. It gives us confidence in our human potential.

48

Caring for Our Mind

We all want peace—in our families, workplaces, and communities. To bring that about, we must take care of our ethical behavior, and to do that, we must take care of our minds.

Avoiding harmful physical and verbal actions is easier than transforming the mind that motivates them. That's why we start with restraining from harmful deeds and words. As our external actions begin to calm down and become more appropriate, we have less regret and guilt, so our minds become clearer. Then we can better monitor our minds, noticing when attachment, anger, confusion, jealousy, arrogance, and so forth creep in, and apply the antidotes to them.

In this book you will find the various antidotes to the different kinds of disturbing emotions and distorted views, so keep reading. As you learn and practice these new ways of thinking and being, over time you'll feel yourself changing. Doing this is actual Dharma practice, and it is never boring!

49

Antidotes to the Afflictions

The Buddha's teachings are full of antidotes to the various mental afflictions that cause our misery and obstruct our spiritual progress. For example, when attachment arises, contemplate impermanence. When anger plagues your mind, cultivate fortitude, the ability to abandon the wish to retaliate when faced with criticism, insults, and even beatings. When hatred burns inside, develop love. When ignorance and confusion stifle you, meditate on the dependent nature of persons and phenomena and dissolve the mistaken notion that things are fixed and rigid. When jealousy attacks, rejoice in the virtue, talents, and opportunities of others. When arrogance is about to push you over a cliff, recall that everything you know, do, and have comes from others, that you were born broke and helpless and have become who you are now due to the kindness of others.

The trick to transforming your mind is to learn the antidotes to the different obstacles and contemplate them when your mind isn't totally under the control of an affliction. In that way, when an affliction arises, you can apply a counterforce to it.

50

Applying the Antidotes

~

Practice the antidotes in your daily meditation and apply them to situations that have occurred in the past or that you think may occur in the future. For example, every morning spend a few minutes thinking, *May all living beings—no matter whether I like them, dislike them, or don't know them—have good health and a peaceful heart and mind.* Become so familiar with this thought that it naturally arises whenever you encounter anyone during the day. This kind thought will balance your mind, prevent hatred, and bring inner peace.

Similarly, train your mind to look at touchy situations from a broad perspective so that your buttons don't get pushed. Best is to dismantle your buttons altogether by constantly training your mind in realistic and beneficial perspectives that free you from self-centeredness and ignorance.

Contemplating an antidote once or twice won't cure you of an affliction forever. You must become habituated with these remedies, and that takes time. The wisdom that realizes emptiness—the ultimate nature of reality—is the antidote to all afflictions, because it sees ourselves and all phenomena as they actually exist, free from our projections on them. Everything is empty of all the false ways of existing that we have projected on them.

51

Mind in the Dharma, Feet on the Earth

Sometimes we meet "spiritual" people who hold the attitude, *Forget this world. Everything's totally screwed up. I'm going to actualize a trance state that's totally unrelated to what's going on here.*

Spiritual practice isn't about escaping from the world; it's about learning to live in it with a wise and compassionate perspective that brings harmony in our lives and the lives of others. We aim to be of great service and benefit to the world. A state of deep concentration is a nice break from a crazy world, but it doesn't last forever. Plus, a trance state isn't liberation; it will eventually end, and we'll find ourselves back where we started. The proper motivation for cultivating single-pointed concentration is to be able to use it as a tool to improve all our other Dharma practices.

The spiritual people I respect the most are humble. They cultivate compassion and wisdom and don't try to impress anyone with how spiritually advanced they are or how many far-out spiritual visions they have had. Instead, with compassion, they don't hesitate to help others, and with wisdom, they know how to help them skillfully. Wouldn't it be liberating to be free of self-centeredness and self-doubt?

52

"Yes, but . . ."

"Yes, but . . ." This is how we agree that something is true or good, but then try to get out of doing it by providing exceptions or making excuses. "Yes, it's good if I do a daily meditation practice, but I have to do x-y-z, which makes it impossible."

Welcome to the book of 35,929,618 excuses. Who benefits from our "yes, but . . ."? Who is harmed by it? What mental factors are running the show?

53

Advice for Difficult Relationships

Sometimes we feel cornered by others' expectations of us, or trapped by our negative feelings toward someone, or tangled up in feeling obliged, or desperately attached to someone and fear separation from them.

When these states of mind arise, it's helpful to think that neither we nor the other person is something fixed. We are not solid, discreet personalities who always have the same roles and relationships. We are constantly changing entities. We didn't have this relationship with this particular person in previous lives and we won't in future lives. And when we do meet again, we'll have a different kind of relationship because conditions will be different and so will our personalities.

Thinking in this way gives us mental space and enables us to treat the other person with respect instead of wrestling with our solid conception of who they are, who we are, and how things between us should be.

54

Repaying the Kindness of Others

Does repaying the kindness of others entail doing whatever others want?

Repaying kindness doesn't mean becoming a people-pleaser. Squeezing yourself to become what you think others think you should be just makes you crazy. Furthermore, it's impossible to make others everlastingly happy because they, like you, are beings in cyclic existence with dissatisfied minds.

Repaying kindness means opening our hearts to see that others are just like you. They have feelings like you. They want happiness and don't want to suffer, just like you. In situations where you can be of direct benefit, take action. In addition, actively practice the path to improve the quality of your own mind. In this way, you'll be able to introduce others to the Dharma and guide them on the path to true happiness.

That's the best way to repay kindness.

55

There Are No Shortcuts

If we don't receive teachings from a reliable guide like the Buddha, we may make up our own path to practice. We've done that in many previous lifetimes, but where has it gotten us? On the other hand, we shouldn't blindly follow the Buddha's teachings. He instructed us to examine his teachings using reasoning to see if they explain our experiences and the world around us, and to practice them to see if they work.

Through hearing, thinking, and meditating, we integrate our minds with the Buddha's teachings so that the Dharma is no longer outside of us, but internalized into our lives. This takes practice and time. There are no shortcuts in this process. But no matter how long it takes, it's worthwhile.

56

A Balanced Attitude

~

As we start to understand that preparing for future lives is more important than chasing sense pleasures in this life, we'll experience more satisfaction in this life. However, don't go to the opposite extreme of shunning this life— giving away all your possessions, depriving your body, or shunning the people you're close to. That doesn't benefit you or others and only causes more problems.

Instead, use your body, possessions, and relationships to create virtue by practicing generosity, ethical conduct, fortitude, joyous effort, concentration, and wisdom. Instead of being attached to the things of this life, use them to create merit—for example, using your possessions to create merit through generosity; seeing your friends, relatives, colleagues, and acquaintances as beings worthy of compassion; and cultivating fortitude, the ability to not retaliate when others harm you. In this way, approach life with a balanced attitude free of clinging or aversion.

57

Bad Moods

~

We get into a bad mood when we want things to be different from the way they are and are unable to accept what's happening. No matter how much we fume, sulk, or complain, things are the way they are, and what's happening is already happening. Rejecting the reality of the present is useless.

If we don't like what's happening, let's reflect on the law of karma and its effects and see that our present experiences are the result of our previous actions in this or previous lives. Rather than reject what's happening now, let's accept it; it's impermanent and will change. What is, is. Apply compassion and wisdom to the situtaion, and let go of the bad mood. With a peaceful heart, smile at the people around you (or at least don't scowl at them)!

58

The Best Motivation

A Dharma motivation looks beyond the happiness of this life to having a fortunate rebirth and eventually attaining liberation or full awakening. Some people might think that such a motivation takes us away from the present into some vague future. This is not the case. These Dharma motivations enhance the importance of this life because we can attain those Dharma aims during this life.

To have a fortunate rebirth, we must diminish our gross afflictions. To attain liberation, we must eliminate all afflictions. And to become a fully awakened buddha, we must purify the mind of all obscurations and cultivate all good qualities. To accomplish these aims, we must live vividly in the present moment, because the only moment in which to practice the Dharma is the present one.

Instead of dreaming of the things you desire or raging over what someone else did—all of which takes us away from the present—focus on cultivating merit and wisdom by transforming the present into the path to joy. Recognize your great fortune at meeting the Buddha's teachings and take delight in creating the causes for happiness for yourself and others.

59

Connecting with a Qualified Spiritual Mentor

Forming a healthy relationship with a qualified spiritual mentor is essential. Books can't inspire us in the same way that an actual human being who practices the path can. Nor can books point out our mistaken actions at the right moment, whereas our teacher can. If we need good teachers in order to learn common skills like driving or typing, we certainly need them for much more delicate and complex activities like transforming our minds.

When we have a relationship of respect and trust with a qualified spiritual mentor, we take their teachings to heart and do our best to practice them. In the process, our faults come to an end and our good qualities increase. In addition, we also create the conditions that enable us to meet qualified spiritual mentors in future lives.

Conversely, if we follow an unqualified teacher, we create destructive karma that will ripen in unfortunate rebirths, and we may be separated from wise and compassionate spiritual mentors in many future lives.

60

Trusting the Three Jewels

We can be sure that the Three Jewels won't betray us because the Buddha was propelled by great compassion to realize the nature of reality. He has no self-centered motivation to harm or manipulate us, and there is no reason whatsoever for him to lie.

Nonetheless, we're easily misled by worldly spirits or psychics. When a fortune-teller predicts that we will fall ill, we immediately do purification practices. But when the Buddha warns of the destructive karma we've created that will ripen in illness, we feel no hurry to purify.

We should know what we believe and why we believe it. Learning about the qualities of the Buddha, Dharma, and Sangha makes our faith in them stable because we examine the teachings and gain conviction in them. Otherwise, someone may come along and teach a philosophy that sounds good but is full of flaws, and we follow him or her down the slippery slope of wrong views.

61

Unexpected Spiritual Teachers

There you are, in a staff meeting or at a family gathering, and some loudmouthed jerk trashes you in front of everybody.

In such situations, there aren't many alternatives. You can go into a rage, cry, or work with your mind.

Although your self-centered mind can't see this jerk as your spiritual teacher, from a Dharma viewpoint they are. Why? You aren't mad at this person for the benefit of all sentient beings, but because they're interfering with your happiness. If you have such a dramatic reaction to somebody smearing your reputation, clearly you're attached to your public image. This person has become your spiritual teacher because they force you to look at your self-centered mind and attachment to reputation, to recognize the "me" whose self-confidence just went out the window because of a few harsh words. Having seen the dirt in your mind, you now know what you need to clean up.

62

A False Friend

The self-centered thought that says, *My happiness is more important than anyone else's, and my suffering hurts more than theirs*, appears to be our friend looking out for our own happiness, but actually it's the source of your misery.

The strong focus on ourselves makes us overly sensitive to others' words and easily offended. Seeing the world through the lens of what helps and harms *me*, we're easily distracted, suspicious, and moody. In the long term, this self-centered thought brings misery because it lies behind all our destructive karma. Needless to say, it destroys others' happiness as well.

Fortunately, the self-centered thought is not who we are; it's not an inherent part of us and can be removed. Seeing how it prevents our happiness, we can counter it by contemplating the benefits of cherishing others, wishing them happiness, and actively working to benefit them. We can practice caring for others in all activities every day—not just in the meditation hall, but as we interact with everybody.

63

Happiness Is for Everyone

Some people believe that to be compassionate, they must suffer. Is this true?

The dichotomy between being happy ourselves and being compassionate toward others is present in Western culture on many levels, but it's not found in Buddhism. The Buddhist perspective is a win-win situation. Working for the welfare of everyone gives us an inner sense of satisfaction that is much greater than selfishly working for our own well-being and ignoring others. Plus, when those around us are happy, our lives go better too. What happiness do we really get from bragging about our own accomplishments if we live near others who are suffering?

When we're kind to ourselves, it's easier to be kind to others. When we're kind to others, it's easier to be kind to ourselves. Let's look out for everyone's happiness and create a better society.

64

Stopping Harm

When we engage in actions that harm others and ourselves, we need to stop and look at what's happening in our minds.

Are we oblivious to what we're doing? If so, we must restore mindfulness of our actions.

Are we unaware that our actions are harmful? If so, we must study the Dharma to learn to discern beneficial from harmful actions.

Are we reckless because we're getting what we want right now? If so, we must cultivate conscientiousness and think about the effects of our actions on ourselves and others.

Are we aware that our actions or words are harmful, but are overwhelmed by attachment, animosity, or confusion? If so, we must apply and strengthen the antidotes to these afflictions so they don't overpower our minds and control our behavior.

65

Keeping Our Hearts Open

Let's strive to cultivate love and compassion for other living beings regardless of whether they're receptive to our help and advice.

When we see someone going down the wrong path and there isn't much we can do because they don't want our advice, we can still hold the thought that wishes for their well-being. If we get frustrated or discouraged and give up trying to benefit them, that closes the door to future beneficial interactions. However, if we simply step back and give the other person space, if that person later decides that they want to change, they will feel more comfortable approaching us for help.

Accepting where people are at and what they are capable of at any particular moment is important. Otherwise, we're always going to be battling them with "you need to be who I want you to be." That's a dead-end. If we can't control our own minds, how are we going to make somebody else's mind change?

66

What We Do Matters

I work with the incarcerated and learn a lot from them. One of their biggest ah-ha moments occurs when they realize that their actions matter. Of course, this applies to all of us; we are the same human beings whether we live inside or outside a razor-wire fence. Our actions affect other people's lives and feelings. Our actions affect not only our immediate experiences, but also what we experience in the long term. We have power to cause suffering and to stop suffering. It is up to us to choose which we want to do.

67

The Qualities of Karma

Happiness always comes from virtue, never nonvirtue. Suffering always comes from nonvirtue, never virtue. This is the first quality of karma. Do we recall this when we're about to act in a nonvirtuous manner? When attachment arises, we think only about getting what we want. When anger arises, we think only about eliminating our stress. We don't think about the long-term or even short-term results. Let's slow down and consider the results of our actions.

The second quality of karma is that its results increase. From a small seed, a big tree grows, and from a small action, a big result may come. We may dismiss a lie as a "little white lie," but later it will have a pronounced effect in our lives. We may pass over the opportunity to give to a charity by thinking it's only a small virtuous action, and miss a big opportunity to create merit. Small things matter; paying attention to them makes a difference.

68

How Karma Works

The third quality of karma is: if we don't create the cause, we won't experience the result. There's often a disconnect between our intellectual understanding of karma and our actions. We must watch out for that. Happiness won't come by praying for it, we must act: make offerings to the Three Jewels and to people in need of help; learn, reflect, and meditate on the Buddha's teachings; practice not following the urge to retaliate.

Once karma is created, it doesn't just vanish. This is the fourth quality of karma. If we purify, the ripening of destructive karma will be impeded. (Entries 103–106 explain the four opponent powers to purify destructive karma.) If we get angry or have wrong views, the ripening of virtuous karma will be obstructed.

Just as cause and effect functions in the physical world, it operates in the ethical and spiritual dimensions as well. Our actions influence our long-term well-being.

69

Content with Creating the Causes

We must meditate a lot on karma and its effects and gain some conviction in it, not just some intellectual understanding. Then we must apply our understanding of karma and its effects to our lives and use it to monitor our actions. Noticing the intention to act in a harmful way, we practice restraining ourselves with the thought, *Good, I'm glad I caught myself before I did this harmful action, interefered with others' happiness, and created the cause for my own future suffering.*

We need to nudge ourselves along to create more virtue, knowing that it is the cause of happiness. Don't worry about when the pleasant result will come—just be content with creating that cause, and then let the good cause bring the good result.

70

Cherishing Others

The mind that cherishes others is happy, joyful, and free. We derive happiness right now and create the karma to meet pleasant situations in the future.

This isn't the same as acting out of obligation or trying to please others so that they'll like us. Cherishing others comes from a place inside us that genuinely respects and appreciates others simply because they exist. For example, doing a household chore with the motivation "I hate doing this, but if I don't my partner will be angry" is no fun. Doing the chore because we want someone to praise us is deceptive, and it's a setup for misery if they don't praise us. But doing the chore because we sincerely care about our family members and want them to be happy makes us happy.

Try applying this not only to situations at home, but also in your workplace and neighborhood.

71

Caring for Our Environment

~~~~~

Be aware of your compassionate intention as you move through the day. How do you relate to your environment and the sentient beings in it? Do you expect them to clean up after you? You may not care if your mess is there, but is it kind to leave it there for others to deal with?

Similarly, take care of your mind. Develop a sense of gratitude for the possessions that you have. Be grateful for all the sentient beings in so many different countries who made the things you have and use. Feel kindness toward them, and then show that kindness in how you speak to others and how you care for your common environment. Treat your things well as a practice of mindfulness and compassion.

72

You Tell Me

—

Sometimes people ask me for advice. They seem sincere, so I offer a suggestion. Then they reply, "Yes, but . . ." So I offer a second solution and am met by "Yes, but . . ." again. At that point I wise up and realize that this person isn't ready to change. To avoid wasting my time and theirs, I turn it back to them and say, "You are an intelligent person and know your situation better than I do. What ideas do you have for how to deal with it?"

The conversation ends there, but I hope my question will make them think.

73

The Most Important One

Although we may not think of ourselves as particularly self-centered, upon investigation we discover that our thoughts and actions center on *I*, *me*, *my*, and *mine*. Although we're too polite to say it out loud, we believe that the world owes us something, that others are on the planet to serve us. Guess what? Everyone else has the same idea, so conflict will inevitably occur!

The self-centered thought tries to get others to side with us against somebody we don't like. It seeks revenge for actual or perceived harms. It gets jealous and is easily offended. It feels inferior and puts on a show to try to convince others and ourselves that we're worthwhile. Who needs the self-centered thought? We certainly don't.

We're not bad people for being selfish, but seeing how self-centeredness inflicts harm on ourselves and others, let's drop it like a hot potato.

74

Arrogance and Low Self-Esteem

We usually think that arrogant people have a puffed-up image of themselves. Actually, they suffer from low self-esteem. If we didn't think we were inferior, we wouldn't put on such a big show to try to convince ourselves and others how competent we are.

Those with genuine self-confidence are humble. They don't need high status or others' praise to believe in themselves.

Rejoicing in our own virtue is important, it's not conceit. We have talents and abilities. Let's rejoice in them and use them to benefit society. We don't need to be best to live a meaningful life.

75

Self-Hatred and Self-Respect

~~~~~~

Low self-esteem and self-hatred are based on incorrect thinking. *I'm the worst one.* Is that really true? *I can't do anything right.* Isn't that an exaggeration? *No one loves me.* All of us have people who care about us.

Write down your self-talk. Then go through each statement and ask yourself, *Is this true or is it an exaggeration?* Drop all the lies and exaggerations—believing them inhibits all the good we can do.

76

Avoid Trading Short-Term Happiness for Long-Term Misery

Any suffering we experience such as an unfortunate birth or physical and mental pain in this life comes about because of negative actions we've done earlier in this life or in previous lives. When we understand that our suffering is due to our own past actions, we stop blaming those involved in our present suffering. We learn from our situation and decide not to accumulate more negative karma that could lead to similar suffering in future lives.

We might think that our present life is worth protecting even at the cost of killing, stealing, or lying. Yet there's no guarantee such actions will preserve this life, which we're going to lose eventually. At the time of death, we bring to our next life the negative karma we created to preserve this life. We may end up trading a short period of happiness in this life for a long period of misery in a future life.

77

Grade AAA Happiness

The transient happiness we experience in cyclic existence is Grade F happiness—it's here, then it's gone. It depends on external people, situations, and things that are changeable. Those who have attained full awakening are trying to help us open our minds so we can attain happiness that isn't just a souvenir hanging on the wall, a trophy on the bookshelf, or photos in a slideshow at the end of our lives. True happiness comes from freeing our minds from afflictions and polluted karma, from generating bodhicitta, and from knowing that the life of each and every sentient being is meaningful in the long-term.

Such Grade AAA happiness is within our reach.

78

Turning to Bodhicitta

~

Our practice takes on a whole different flavor when we cultivate the altruistic intention of bodhicitta, the mind that seeks to attain full awakening in order to benefit all sentient beings most effectively. We commit ourselves to going in that direction when we adopt the bodhisattva ethical code. Bodhisattvas are those who have familiarized themselves with this intention to such an extent that it arises spontaneously in their minds, and bodhisattva precepts guide their behavior. The wonderful, long-term, altruistic motivation of bodhicitta helps us to overcome obstacles on the path.

Bodhicitta is very helpful for dealing with our two-year-old minds of attachment that scream, *I want this, I want that*, or our rebellious teenager minds that snap, *Why are you telling me what to do?* or our adult minds that whine, *After all I've done for you, look how you're treating me!*

Turning our minds to bodhicitta inspires us to drop whatever self-centered drama we're stuck in at the moment.

79

Examining Our Habits

Without even trying, we recognize others' habits. If we see people regularly, their habitual ways of thinking, feeling, speaking, and acting become evident to us; but our own habits are not so obvious to us. Or sometimes they're obvious, but we're entrenched in them. We defend them. We don't want to change them. What a recipe for suffering!

Instead of using a microscope to examine others' faults, it's better to use a mirror and see our own. The Buddha said, "Look not so much at what other people do and leave undone, but at your own actions, what you do and leave undone."

Dharma practice involves getting to know ourselves very well—looking at our habits and evaluating which ones lead to long-term happiness and which ones lead to misery. Then we learn the techniques the Buddha taught—many of which are found in this book—to subdue the ones that aren't beneficial and to enhance and maintain the ones that are.

80

Who Says I'm Defensive?

We get bent out of shape when we think others are criticizing us. We have such a hard time accepting negative feedback and want to explain ourselves and defend our choices. Even when a friend gives us wise advice, it's so hard for us to listen, say "thank you," and then think about what they said. Everything becomes a discussion or a litigation. It's exhausting.

Similarly, if someone in a meeting says something we disagree with, an uncontrollable urge often arises in us to correct what they said, as if the existence of the world depended on vanquishing their wrong idea. Instead, this often calls attention to their idea. Whereas if we just sit back and let the discussion continue, often no one takes up their idea and it fades away without the need to create a commotion about it.

81

Our Real Problem

When we complain about our likes, dislikes, and difficulties, or even about crises like losing a limb, losing a relative, or dying, it's quite helpful to remember that our real problem is that we're in cyclic existence. We're born with a body and mind under the control of afflictions and karma.

When we pay attention to the real problem, minor annoyances and even major upsets recede into the background. They don't disturb our minds because our attention is focused on creating the causes for ourselves—and by extension others—to be free from cyclic existence. Shifting our orientation to what is really important, our minds become more peaceful.

82

Responding to Betrayal

~

When someone we've cared for betrays our trust, this is an opportunity to reflect on times we've done something similar by treating those who've cared for us like enemies. Growing up, we didn't always appreciate our parents, and we probably gave them lots of headaches. Now when we're on the receiving end of ingratitude, the boomerang has returned and hit us. This gives us an opportunity to regret our previous actions and make amends by apologizing to those whose trust we've betrayed or whose kindness we've taken for granted.

A child with a raging fever may be delirious and kick, scream, and call his mother names. Understanding that the child is out of control due to fever, the mother doesn't take this behavior personally and instead looks on her child with love. In the same way we can look with love and compassion at those who betray our trust because we understand that their mind is overwhelmed by afflictions.

83

Bodhisattvas Wash Others' Dishes

Your friend, housemate, or spouse leaves a few dirty dishes in the sink, and you angrily think, *Why are they so inconsiderate? Do they think I'm their servant?* But if we practice the Dharma, at that moment we'll pause and reflect with honesty: *Hmm, I think I'm too good to clean up someone else's mess, and as much as I talk about and appreciate love, my love doesn't stretch far enough to wash their dishes. This is pride, an attitude that sabotages my ethical conduct.*

Try changing your attitude even more: *I want to be like the bodhisattvas who see themselves as the servants of others. This person who left the dirty dishes in the sink has been kind to me in previous lives. What's so bad about washing their dishes? It only takes two minutes, whereas my aggravation due to the story I'm telling myself consumes an hour of my time.*

Real practice means noticing afflictions as they arise and transforming our mind by seeing the situation from a different perspective, and responding to it with kindness and compassion.

84

Faith

~~~~~~

I used to compare myself to fellow Dharma practitioners. They had so much faith; they saw our teachers as buddhas and praised them constantly. They showed no doubt in the Dharma, whereas I was full of doubts and questioned things constantly. *I'll never get anywhere*, I thought, even though I knew I couldn't will myself to have the kind of faith my friends had.

But decades later, I'm still here, still following the same teachers, loving the Dharma as I did before. Some of those friends with seemingly unshakable faith have disappeared. How foolish I was to compare myself to others!

85

Poison to Our Practice

The great meditators say that attachment to food is easy to let go of, but attachment to reputation is much more difficult to release. We can abide in a solitary retreat place and be content with the simple food we eat, but constantly ponder, *I wonder what people in town think of me. Do they know I'm an ascetic striving for awakening? Are they aware of the deep insights I have? When my retreat is over, they will all come to receive teachings from me. I'll have a new title and will be holy. They'll give me many offerings to show their respect.*

Such thoughts are very seductive; they poison our practice and destroy a good motivation. The point of Dharma practice is to purify the mind of ignorance, anger, attachment, arrogance, and jealousy, and to enhance our good qualities.

86

Worldly Fortune Is without Essence

The Buddha warned about the ego problems and power trips that can arise if we become rich, famous, and well-respected. To counteract this, we need to meditate on the transient, essenceless nature of worldly fortune.

Having worldly fortune doesn't mean we're a good person or an excellent practitioner. Unlike merit created by virtuous deeds, renown and wealth cannot follow us to our future lives. Seeking fame and fortune, we may easily become conceited or complacent in our spiritual practice.

Until we attain full awakening, we are students and disciples. His Holiness the Dalai Lama tells us that he views himself as an older Dharma brother who shares what he knows with others. If he sees himself this way, certainly we, who lack even a fraction of his qualities, should see ourselves with a humble attitude.

87

Cherishing Life

All beings cherish their own lives more than anything else. Still, when human beings are overwhelmed by emotions or wrong views, they are blind to this fact and justify killing animals or even people. Some religious interpretations say that animals were created for human benefit so it's fine to kill them. Some people think that sacrificing animals appeases the gods. Still others think that killing nonbelievers brings rewards in heaven. These are all examples of ignorance.

That killing occurs due to anger is obvious. Sometimes people kill the very people they're most attached to, such as in situations of domestic violence. When we are very attached to someone, our anger toward them becomes equally strong. To free ourselves of that anger, we must diminish our attachment before it leads to harmful consequences. Remembering that other people are not our possessions and nourishing our sense of inner security decreases our attachment and dependence on others to fulfill our emotional needs.

If we want to contribute to world peace, one of the first things to do is to stop harming others physically, especially by taking their lives. Just as each of us sees our own life as most precious, so do all other living beings.

88

Confusion about the Cause of Happiness

~

For my twenty-first birthday, my friends took me to a nice seafood restaurant. There were many lobsters in a glass container, and we could pick out the one we wanted to eat. The chef would then drop it live into boiling water. I thought of myself as a kind person. It never dawned on me that this living being would experience excruciating suffering. Later, when I encountered the Buddha's teachings, I had great regret not only for causing that lobster pain, but also for putting the seed of the destructive deed of killing on my mindstream. I pray to be able to benefit whatever living being that lobster became in its next life.

89

Drinking Salt Water

Drinking salt water to quench our thirst only makes us thirstier. Likewise, the more we indulge in what we crave, the more our dissatisfaction increases because the happiness that worldly things provide is very brief.

Not having what we crave is not a source of unhappiness; craving is. Without craving, we are free—we are satisfied whether or not we possess those desirable people or items.

The antidotes to craving are many, such as seeing that the transient objects we crave cannot bring lasting satisfaction. Contemplating the disadvantages of craving—for example, it interferes with generating bodhicitta and causes distraction when we meditate—is also helpful.

Overcoming craving occurs gradually. We begin by identifying what we're most attached to and slowly but consistently chip away at that attachment, experiencing more mental peace as we do.

90

My Anger Is Realistic

~

Anger is a mental factor that is based on the exaggeration or projection of a bad quality onto someone or something, making us want to harm it or get away from it. By definition, anger is unrealistic because it's based on exaggeration and projection. Yet when we're angry, we don't think, *My mind isn't perceiving reality. Instead we think, I'm perceiving this situation 100 percent correctly. The resolution of this conflict is simple—I'm right; you're wrong and you must change and do things my way.*

How much trouble we cause ourselves with our stubborn insistence on always being right! And where does it get us? Realizing that anger is based on a distorted conception enables us to put it down. Then there's space in our minds for a realistic and beneficial attitude.

91

The Strength to Say "Sorry"

Pride often prevents us from admitting our mistakes, even when both we and the other person know we made them. We feel we'll lose face by apologizing. We fear the other person will have power over us if we admit our mistake. To defend ourselves, we attack, diverting the attention away from ourselves and to the other person. This strategy is commonly practiced on kindergarten playgrounds as well as in national and international politics.

Contrary to our fearful misconceptions, apologizing indicates inner strength, not weakness. We have enough honesty and self-confidence that we don't need to pretend to be faultless. Often all the other person wants is for us to acknowledge their pain. So many tense situations can be defused with the simple, sincere words, "My behavior or words disappointed me and caused you pain. I'm sorry."

92

The Recipient of Kindness

Throughout our lives we have received kindness. The proof is that we are still alive. Without others' care and efforts, we would have died long ago. People took care of us when we were infants, gave us an education, and encouraged our abilities. Strangers constructed the buildings we live in, and grew and transported the food we eat. Now more than any other time in human history we depend on one another to stay alive and to thrive.

Understanding that we have been the recipient of great kindness throughout our lives enables us to connect to other living beings with the urge to repay the kindness or to pay it forward. Not only do others contribute to our well-being, but we also have an opportunity to contribute to theirs.

Let's take joy in bringing happiness to others.

93

The Judgmental Mind

When we get together with friends and discuss others' faults, our conclusion is that we are better than they are. This is a rather silly way to increase our self-esteem, isn't it?

To counteract our judgmental mind, let's own the fact that we do the very things we're criticizing others for doing, or we might have done them in previous lives even if we haven't done them in this life. As long as afflictions inhabit our minds, we're capable of doing anything.

What we notice in others is often what we don't like about ourselves. Rather than criticize the other person, it's better to think that they are showing us how we look when we act that way. That helps us change our ways.

94

Appreciating Our Beauty

Each of us comes into this world with unique talents, dispositions, and interests. We should recognize that and use our abilities for the benefit of all beings. Instead of trying to make all beings fit into the same round hole, especially if they are triangular or star-shaped, let's give everyone an opportunity to appreciate the beauty of their own shape and use their talents and abilities to contribute to the welfare of all.

95

Survival of the Most Cooperative

Western culture is based on ideas of rugged individualism and competition. We think that survival of the fittest breeds competence and ignore the pain and tragedy competition leaves in its wake. But if our species is to continue, if as individuals we are going to thrive, we must acknowledge how much we depend on one another and realize that mutual cooperation is essential. Ants and bees cooperate for the welfare of their entire anthill or hive. Surely, with our human intelligence, we can cooperate for the benefit of all.

96

The Greatest Generosity

~~~~~~

We can be generous in so many ways—giving material goods, time, service, protection, encouragement, and affection. It is said that the gift of the Dharma excels all others. This may consist of teaching the Dharma, leading discussion groups, guiding meditations, giving spiritual counseling, and speaking of Dharma antidotes to non-Buddhists without using Buddhist jargon. After all, so many of the Buddha's teachings are common sense and are free of doctrinal beliefs.

97

Helping Relatives Meet the Teachings

Young adults often ask me, "How can I get my family interested in the Dharma?" I reply, "Take out the garbage."

Think about it: Mom has been asking to you take out the garbage for eighteen to thirty years. You come home after a Buddhist retreat or course and take out the garbage, and Mom says, "Wow! I've been trying for years to get my son/daughter to take out the garbage. They attend a Buddhist event and finally do it. Buddhism is fantastic!"

Another way is to leave easy-to-understand Dharma books that talk about love, compassion, and forgiveness around the house. Don't point them out—just let your family members pick them up when they are so inclined.

98

Being an Activist

As we continue to cultivate compassion and the altruistic intention of bodhicitta, we may also have the urge to express them in concrete ways in our lives. Some people may do this by caring for a sick relative; others may do it by working for systemic change in their corporate workplace or in the justice system; and still others may express their compassion by working in an animal shelter, registering people to vote, or building wells in Africa. Humankind needs all of these contributions. We can't say one is better than another, because the value of each act depends on the strength of our virtuous motivation.

What is similar in all these cases is the importance of living in a balanced way so that we can continue to serve. We must take time for ourselves to physically rest and to spiritually rejuvenate. There will always be more to do, so rejoicing at what we are able to do is more valuable than pushing ourselves to the point of exhaustion.

99

Bearing Sadness and Grief without Self-Reproach

A man in his thirties came to Sravasti Abbey where I live, with the intention of straightening out his life. Jeff (not his real name) had been a junkie and was now clean. He loved the Dharma and worked hard offering service. After a few months he wanted to go back home to try living what he had learned about the Dharma there. We were skeptical of the wisdom of his decision but accepted it.

Jeff kept in touch with us off and on, and we learned after a few months that he was shooting up again. His family did all they could to support him in rehab, and so did we. But after several months he overdosed. Our sadness was great. One of his friends began to "what if," saying that he had planned to call Jeff that weekend but had forgotten to. He wondered if perhaps Jeff would still be alive today if only he had remembered to call him.

Such self-blame is useless. So many people had tried to help Jeff for a very long time, but the force of the addictive mind was too strong and he couldn't grab onto one of the life rafts his family and friends had sent his way.

Now our job is to engage in virtuous actions and dedicate the merit for Jeff's rebirth. Through the power of putting effort into our Dharma practice, may we advance on the path and share the Buddha's liberating teachings with Jeff in his future lives.

The Foundation of Our Well-Being

Sometimes beginners and even people who have been practicing awhile fancy themselves advanced practitioners and want to practice Tantra, Mahamudra, and Dzogchen. However, when their teacher gives instructions on the five precepts and encourages them to stop lying, sleeping around, or drinking and drugging, they get really put off, saying those are beginners' practices.

But if you think carefully, keeping ethical conduct is not that easy. Look at how many people in high positions in entertainment, sports, politics, business, and finance are called out for their lack of basic morality. To have a pure intention and avoid all harm requires considerable training.

Ethical conduct is the basis for generating the aspiration for liberation, bodhicitta, and the wisdom that realizes emptiness. Those three are the necessary basis for the advanced practices of Tantra, Mahamudra, and Dzogchen.

To build a sturdy and beautiful house, we need to lay a solid foundation and erect strong walls before constructing the roof. Building a firm and competent Dharma practice is similar.

101

Keeping the Precepts

~

Precepts—the basis of ethical conduct—are very precious. To actualize the Buddha's teachings, we must start with the basics: subduing our harmful verbal and physical actions. By keeping the five lay precepts (or if we're ordained, the monastic precepts), we increase our mindfulness of how we want to be in the world and sharpen our introspective awareness, which observes whether we're living in accord with our values and precepts. Strengthening mindfulness and introspective awareness positively affects our meditation because these two mental factors are necessary to cultivate concentration, and thus are important to stabilize bodhicitta and wisdom.

Life Review

~

Doing a life review centered on the ten nonvirtues helps us make peace with the past. These ten are: killing, stealing, sexual misconduct, lying, divisive speech, harsh speech, idle talk, covetousness, malice, and wrong views. Don't criticize yourself for having done these, but do make an effort to understand your actions and your motivations for doing them so you can change in the future.

Examine the times when you've engaged in these ten nonvirtuous actions and reflect, *What was my mental state? What did I think I was going to achieve by doing this? How did I feel afterward? What will I do if a similar situation arises in the future?*

103

Purification: Regret

~

Some of our psychological malaise—guilt, self-hatred, and so forth—originates from our involvement in the ten nonvirtues. To remedy this and start afresh, purification with the four opponent powers is very helpful and refreshing. These four are: regretting the destructive action, restoring the relationship, determining to change our ways, and engaging in a remedial action.

First, generate regret for the destructive action. Regret is not guilt. Guilt is exaggerated and self-centered. It dwells on ourselves in a distorted way, seeing our actions as irredeemable and ourselves as thoroughly corrupt. Abandon guilt and instead regret harming others and harming yourself by putting the seeds of destructive karma on your mindstream. Regret owns what is our responsibility without the harshness involved in blame and guilt. This self-honesty is psychologically healthy and releases the energy we have kept bound up in rationalizing, justifying, and blaming.

104

Purification: Restoring the Relationship

Our destructive actions are motivated by our afflictions, and they destroy our relationships with others. Restoring the relationship entails changing our attitude toward whomever we have hurt, by generating love, compassion, and bodhicitta toward all sentient beings, and by taking refuge in the Three Jewels. Directly apologizing to the person we've harmed isn't always necessary, although it may be helpful to meet them or write to them to express our regret and our wish to make amends. The important piece is that we release whatever disturbing emotion we had toward them and cultivate a positive one in its stead.

105

Purification: Determining to Change Our Ways

—

Making a determination to change your behavior steers your energy in a good way. Don't promise yourself that you'll do things you can't yet do. Be realistic—if you are capable of abandoning lying for three days, then promise yourself you'll do that. That way you'll feel successful after not lying for three days.

Don't give up on yourself, thinking, *I'm an angry person who will never be able to control my temper.* That isn't true. First, determine to learn techniques to manage your anger. After learning them, practice them and familiarize yourself with thinking that way when you're not angry. When your mind becomes familiar with these techniques, then practice them in situations you encounter. Slowly, slowly, you'll make progress.

106

Purification: Remedial Action

The fourth opponent power to purify nonvirtuous karma is to engage in virtuous actions. This may be a particular Dharma practice such as bowing to the Buddha and the bodhisattvas, making offerings to them, reciting mantra, and meditating on emptiness or compassion. Or it may involve volunteering at a charity, printing Dharma books for free distribution, serving at an animal shelter, volunteering at a monastery or Dharma center—any action that benefits others.

When you've completed the four opponent powers, release any and all negative mental energy you've had tied up in past destructive actions. Have a sense of freshness and starting anew.

107

Attachment and Aspiration

Based on exaggeration and projection of its good qualities, we cling to a desirable object. Motivated by clinging, we may lie, cheat, or do other nonvirtuous actions to get what we want.

People often ask if it's possible to become attached to awakening. If we understand what awakening is and its benefit, being attracted to it and aspiring to attain it is not attachment, because no exaggeration or projection of excellent qualities is involved. Awakening is a state of limitless excellent qualities. Similarly, aspiring to attain a fortunate rebirth and desiring to cultivate great compassion for all beings are not based on exaggeration or projection and do not motivate negative actions.

We can feel the difference between attachment and a virtuous aspiration in the mood, "texture," or "tone" of our mind. With attachment there's fear of being separated from the desired object or person; we're grasping at something external with the assumption that there is happiness in it. Virtuous aspiration is more grounded. There may be a sense of passion—for example, seeking to benefit sentient beings—that energizes us to work hard to attain our Dharma goals, but our mind is grounded, patient, and free of the desperate hurry that goes with attachment.

108

Wrong Views

———

Wrong view is another nonvirtue that is created mentally. It entails denying the existence of something that exists, such as the law of karma and its effects, the Three Jewels, liberation and full awakening, and our potential to attain them. With erroneous reasons, we stubbornly hold on to such wrong views and are unwilling to even consider other ideas.

Holding wrong views is dangerous because we give ourselves license to do all the other verbal and physical nonvirtues. For example, we may think, *I can do whatever I like as long as no one finds out, because my actions don't have an ethical dimension and won't bring long-term results.*

In Buddhism, we abandon harmful actions not because we're afraid of punishment by either the police or God, but because we respect ourselves and others and don't want any of us to suffer.

109

Transforming Adversity into the Path

When someone criticizes or harms us, we usually think we haven't done anything to deserve this treatment and we may believe this justifies our retaliation.

Whether we've antagonized the other person or not, the fact is that the destructive karma we created by harming someone in the past is now ripening, so there's no sense in being angry at the person harming us now. This doesn't mean that we deserve to suffer, but that the primary cause of our present harm was our own negative deeds done under the influence of self-centeredness in this or a previous life. Rather than waste our energy in anger, we can respond to such experiences by increasing our purification practice to prevent other destructive karma from ripening. We can also meditate on the faults of self-centeredness and the benefits of cherishing others so that we don't create destructive karma in the future.

This is the meaning of transforming adversity into the path to awakening.

The Taking-and-Giving Meditation

Our usual response to people who threaten or harm us is fear and anger. Our knee-jerk reaction that seeks to retaliate is inappropriate, because when we harm somebody who harmed us, they will return the harm, escalating the conflict. Even if we succeed in intimidating them and they succumb, their unhappiness will eventually make them rebel or distance themselves from us. This dynamic plays out in families, groups, and nations. It lies behind so many wars and personal disputes.

To do taking-and-giving meditation, with compassion imagine taking on others' suffering, misdeeds, and afflictions in the form of pollution. This turns into a thunderbolt that destroys the hard lump of self-centeredness at your heart chakra in the center of your chest. From the clear, open space that remains, generate love, wishing the other person to have happiness and its causes. With this motivation, imagine transforming your body, possessions, and merit so that they become whatever the person needs or wants. Give this to them and imagine that they become happy, peaceful, and content. Don't begrudge their well-being; after all, the happier your enemies are, the less likely they are to harm you again.

The best thing we can wish for our enemies is to learn about and begin practicing the Dharma. Imagine what kind and generous people they will become!

III

Activating Wisdom

When with our own wisdom we understand the disadvantages of destructive actions of body, speech, and mind, countering them becomes much easier. Our minds aren't distracted by guilt, believing we are judged, or by rebelliousness when someone asks us to do something. Rather, we understand that we want to be happy and respect our spiritual goals. This necessitates that we change our ways.

We may not be able to change our negative behavior right away, but if we stop justifying or rationalizing it and start familiarizing ourselves with wisdom, gradually change will occur.

High Rebirth and Highest Goodness

Our spiritual goals fall into two categories. The first is a high rebirth as a human or as a god. The second is the highest goodness of liberation, or full awakening. The two are related because we'll need a series of fortunate rebirths to create all the causes for liberation and full awakening. An unfortunate rebirth hinders our opportunities and our ability to learn and practice the Dharma.

Faith is a principal factor to obtain a good rebirth, and wisdom is the primary cause of the highest goodness. Faith refers specifically to the belief in the law of karma and its effects. This is not obvious to us as beginners, so first we must reflect on cause and effect in general, and then see that this refers to our actions and their long-term effects. Cultivating faith in the Buddha also helps, since that makes us more receptive to his teachings on karma and its effects.

The wisdom that liberates us from cyclic existence and leads to the highest goodness is cultivated through reasoning. Hearing teachings and exercising our "mental muscles" is the way to gain that.

113

My Business and Not My Business

There's a lovely verse in the Vinaya (the Buddhist monastic discipline) that goes: "Just as a bee feeding on flowers extracts only their nectar without spoiling their color or fragrance, so a monastic entering a city or village is mindful only of their own behavior to see if it is correct, and does not interfere in others' affairs or inspect what they do or do not do."

My business is what my body, speech, and mind are doing. Do I have a good motivation? Is my speech truthful, kind, encouraging, and appropriate? Are my actions done with care and grace? It is also my business to offer help to anyone I notice needing help. But if my mind starts to comment on others' behavior, finds fault with their speech, imputes intention to their minds, this is not my business. My job is not to be like a sports announcer making a running commentary on what others are doing; it's to be like a bee gathering nectar and pollinating blossoms without doing any harm.

114

Think Before We Speak

Harsh speech occurs when our minds are under the influence of afflictions, and we release tension by insulting and criticizing others. We haven't paused to think about what the other person's concerns may be or how to communicate effectively, so our speech disturbs their mind and causes them to back away. We know this because we react to unskillful speech in exactly the same way.

We often speak harshly because we have interpreted others' actions or speech as aggressive. At those times it is helpful to question our perceptions and check to see if we have understood the other person's meaning correctly. Sometimes we hear just a few words and immediately become defensive, believing that person is challenging or disrespecting us. It's helpful to stop any knee-jerk responses, listen to the other person with an open mind, and then check that we have understood them correctly by repeating to them what we think they are feeling and needing.

115

Making Ourselves the Victim

When there's conflict between two people, it doesn't matter who started it. What matters is how we respond. Our thoughts and behavior are our responsibility no matter what another person did to trigger them. Otherwise, we make ourselves into a victim: "I'm miserable because he did this." "I'm confused and lonely because she did that." This way of thinking makes us believe we have no control over how we feel.

Blaming others is enticing: If I am a victim of others' actions, then I don't have to try to change. I can feel sorry for myself or spray my anger around with impunity.

Actually, it doesn't work that way. No one can make us a victim; we make ourselves a victim. Changing our perspective and learning to release unrealistic and unbeneficial thoughts is the way to freedom.

116

Right and Wrong

Some people view life in terms of right and wrong. I am right, you are wrong. I did something wrong and will be punished. My mistakes mean I'm wrong and make me a bad person. Making rigid categories like this, we judge ourselves and others harshly and become unhappy and bitter.

It's more helpful to think in terms of activities being beneficial or unbeneficial, and views as being realistic or unrealistic. Making a mistake and acting in an unbeneficial way doesn't make you a bad person. Having unrealistic expectations of family, friends, or colleagues doesn't mean you are wrong and bad.

Treat yourself with kindness: admit your mistaken actions or views, make amends, and go on. There's no benefit in seeing yourself as wrong or bad. Doing so is unrealistic; leave that unhelpful habit behind.

117

Accept the Love of Others

Many people feel lonely and unloved, as if they didn't matter to the world or to the people around them: *When I die, no one will care or even notice.* This way of thinking is based on repeating falsehoods to ourselves. Each one of us has many people who care about us, who love us and wish us the best. Often we are blind to their affection. We just don't see it.

Sometimes the way other people show their affection isn't the way we want them to show it. They invite us to dinner and we think they are making demands of us. They point out our good qualities and we believe they are making fun of us. These kinds of distorted thoughts are the result of a self-centered attitude, and we need to call it for what it is.

When we open our eyes, we see that many people love and care about us. Let's open our hearts and accept that love.

118

Making Progress

———

When we begin practicing we may wonder, *Is it possible to get rid of the self-centered thought? Isn't it hardwired into me?*

As we learn mind-training techniques and apply antidotes to the afflictions, over time we can see that we're making progress. We don't get jealous or resentful as much, depression doesn't visit us as often or last as long, and our smile becomes genuine. This gives us confidence in the efficacy of the Dharma based on our own experience. Our self-centered thoughts may not be completely gone, but they're certainly fewer. That's progress that we can rejoice in.

Over time, topics that we initially understood only intellectually become more heartfelt. The concept of emptiness used to be a mystery to us; now, when our concentration and wisdom are stronger, we have some sense that we don't exist in the way we appear to.

119

Practicing in Daily Life

~

Our spiritual practice should be something that relates to our daily lives and the world around us. We aim to transcend the world by eliminating the ignorance, anger, and attachment that bind us, so we can experience the true peace and freedom of full awakening. This transcendental state must be fully applicable to what is happening with sentient beings now. Our purpose is not to disengage from the world and abide in our own state of blissful samadhi, but to free our minds from the afflictions that perpetuate cyclic existence so that we can benefit sentient beings most effectively. Certainly this requires periods of secluded practice free from distraction, but our ultimate purpose is to repay others' kindness by showing them the path to awakening.

120

The Essence of the Buddha's Teachings

A single verse summarizes all the wisdom of the Buddha's 84,000 teachings: "To avoid all wrong; to bring all good to perfection; to fully discipline your mind—this is the Buddha's teaching." The simple sayings, the complex philosophy, the numbered lists—all of these are for the purpose of leading us to abandon all harm, enrich our good qualities to their utmost, and tame our afflictions and mental defilements. We needn't be confused about what to do: our work is cut out for us.

121

Rejoicing

Rejoicing in others' virtue, opportunities, talents, and knowledge is an easy way to be happy and create merit. Rejoicing is also the antidote to jealousy. There's a real joy in rejoicing in others' happiness and attainment, whereas being jealous of them serves only to make us miserable.

I'm glad I'm not the best person in the world because if I were, two problems would arise. First, there would be no one for me to learn from, so I would stagnate. Second, we would all live like Neanderthals because I don't know about electricity, plumbing, construction, engineering, medicine, and so many other fields. I'm glad people know more than I do and have talents that I don't have because the world and I benefit from all of us sharing our knowledge and abilities.

122

Rules of the Universe

I have many rules of the universe, rules that I expect every-one to know and honor, even though they have no idea what they are.

The first rule is that everyone has to think well of me and like me. No one is allowed to dislike me.

Second, no one is allowed to criticize me. Everyone must praise me.

Third, everyone must do what I want them to do, when I want them to do it. No stepping out of line here!

I could go on and on with my rules, but I'll spare you.

No wonder I have problems with other people . . .

Do you have any rules of the universe?

123

The Judge and Jury

⁓

When we're angry at someone, the law-enforcement officials occupy our mind. First, as the sheriff, we arrest the
person who has made us angry: "You're arrested under
the charge of criticizing me in public. That is a major vio-
lation of my laws of the universe." As the prosecutor, we
file charges against the person. There is no defense because
he or she is undoubtedly guilty. The jury also exists in our
mind and it votes unanimously to punish this person. The
judge then condemns the person to life in the prison of
"people I hate the most."

Does any of this make us happy? Is this the meaning of
justice?

124

The Wish to Practice

As we become familiar with the Buddhist worldview and develop the sincere intention to practice the Dharma, we naturally see that harmful actions are antithetical to our wholesome goals. We change our thoughts, words, and actions, not because external regulations are imposed on us, not because we fear punishment, and not to win others' approval, but because our earnest wish to abandon negativity and cultivate virtue comes from within our hearts.

The entire Buddhist path must be practiced in this way. The wish to transform our minds comes from our side, not because we should, we're supposed to, we ought to, we're obligated to, or somebody's going to think poorly of us if we don't, but because deep in our hearts is the genuine aspiration to complete the path.

125

Meeting a Moose

One afternoon, a friend and I were walking in the Sravasti Abbey forest when we came upon a moose on the path. He trotted away from us shyly, then turned and looked at us as intently as we looked at him.

We share a universe with so many different kinds of sentient beings, all of whom have been our parents in previous lives. When we meet them again in this life, instead of just seeing them as who they appear to be now, we can think, *That's someone I've been very close to in the past, someone who's been kind to me.*

Whether we see moose, grasshoppers, somebody we like, or someone we fear, if we see them as someone just like us, who wants happiness and not suffering, it pulls us out of our solid view of them and gives us a way to relate to them with kindness.

126

Being Special

—

From one angle, each of us is special: we have our unique karmic situation, our particular talents and interests. From another angle, we aren't special at all: each of us wants happiness and not suffering; each of us is bound in cyclic existence by afflictions and karma; each of us has the potential to become a buddha.

Our self-centered thought wants us to be special. We may fancy ourselves to be undiscovered masters with profound realizations who have taken rebirth in the world. For people to think this is a philosophy that refutes the existence of an independent "I" is rather humorous and effectively proves that in fact we are not realized masters. Free from grasping at an inherently existent self, great masters lack arrogance.

It's completely okay not to be special. We don't have to prove ourselves, nor should we compete to be better practitioners than others. Being ordinary in this respect allows us to relax.

127

Hypocrisy

The law of karma and its effects doesn't allow for hypocrisy. Putting on a face to convince others that we are learned, athletic, artistic, intelligent, and so forth doesn't mean we are, nor does it create the causes to be that. The karma we create at any given moment depends principally on the degree to which our motivation is virtuous.

Having said that, "fake it till you make it" in our practice has some value, because in doing so we consciously try to engage in virtue that will transform our minds. This is very different than hypocritically trying to *appear* like good practitioners.

It's important to continually check to see if we're trying to cover up what's really going on inside by looking good, or if we're getting complacent or arrogant in our practice. Then, with kindness and compassion for ourselves, we correct our motivation.

128

Pampering the Body

~

Some of us obsess about our body, thinking it must always be healthy. *I must exercise this much every day. I need special clothes and a helmet to go cycling. These must be color-coordinated and show off my figure.* If we stub our toe, we cry out in pain as if no other human being has ever experienced such pain. When it's very cold, we're afraid of getting sick and bundle up; when it's too hot, we fear we'll faint from the heat.

On and on we worry about this body. In fact, our whole world can be condensed down to the welfare of this body. Worry and anxiety become the (polluted) air we breathe, and our Dharma practice is buried under the weight of fear regarding what will happen to this body.

We are not our bodies. The mind temporarily occupies this body, like a guest staying in a hotel. Understanding this, we accept the transient nature of the body. We keep it healthy and clean and use it wisely to engage in Dharma practice.

129

Becoming a Doctor to Your Mind

Having the motivation to become a doctor is the first step to becoming one, but it isn't sufficient to make it a reality. Similarly, having the motivation to overcome afflictions is good, but it won't prevent them from arising. We must act. To become a doctor, you must attend medical school. To overcome afflictions, you need to be vigilant in guarding your mind. Taking a break from your usual environment to go deeper into your Dharma practice is very helpful to develop antidotes to the afflictions. For this reason, it's good to attend a meditation retreat or course every year.

130

Training Our Mental Muscles

—

It's difficult to stop our afflictions from arising unless we're well-practiced in their antidotes. At the beginning of our practice we are slow to notice the afflictions, or we don't know the antidote to apply to the affliction that has manifested, or we know the antidote but forget to apply it. Nonetheless, we keep coming back to our practice since we're trying to counteract habitual tendencies that have existed since beginningless time.

Applying antidotes to the afflictions is like training our muscles for an athletic event. They're weak at first but get stronger if we keep practicing with patience and consistency and don't get discouraged. Results will come if we have a long-term perspective and are willing to put in the energy to change our mind.

131

Good and Bad Habits

~

Based on karma we've created in previous lives, we have a tendency to repeat the same patterns in this life. Looking at our lives, we can see certain virtuous actions that we do easily, or virtuous mental states that arise easily. These are the results of having established these patterns in previous lives and therefore having that habitual energy. We can thank whomever we were in a previous life for those parts of ourselves that are virtuous and easier to activate.

Then we have nonvirtuous habits that we're also well-trained in. That's because in a previous life we didn't try to counteract them. We just kept doing them, and now the habit continues. It's important in this life to try and deal with our habitual negative tendencies, so we don't carry them into future lives.

132

Medicine for the Mind

When you are filled with desire, imagine getting whatever you're craving and having it year after year. Will the satisfaction of your desires make you happy when you're dying?

When anger arises, meditate on fortitude, the strength of mind that will enable us to bear adversity and remain calm in the face of suffering. This can prevent the compounded misery of getting angry because you're suffering, feeling guilty because you're angry, then becoming depressed because you're feeling guilty.

When you're jealous, rejoicing in someone's good qualities and happiness is the last thing you may want to do, but you must deal with your mind as if it's a screaming child.

For arrogance, reflect on the fact that all your knowledge, skills, and abilities have depended on the kindness of others who taught you—there's nothing there that's yours alone.

If you understand that all persons and phenomena lack independent existence, meditating on that is the best antidote for all the afflictions.

133

Mindfulness in Every Moment

———

It's crucial to observe your mind moment by moment to see if it's in a virtuous, nonvirtuous, or neutral state. You have this precious human life for just a short time, so every moment is important for creating the causes for future happiness for yourself and others. Dharma practice isn't just what you do on the meditation cushion. Your mindfulness and introspective awareness must extend to what's going on in your mind throughout the day.

If someone asks you what you thought about while you drove to work, jogged, or washed the car, would you be able to tell them? Being mindful of what is wholesome and introspectively monitoring your thoughts are important during all activities.

134

Rainy Days

~

We may have many opinions about rain: "I love to hear the sound of raindrops." "I can't stand how muddy it gets when it rains." "Thank goodness we're finally getting some rain." "Ugh, I can't go running today."

A different way to see rain that increases our wisdom is to view it as the product of causes and conditions, and as a cause that produces future results. The line "April showers bring May flowers" (that produce wilted flowers in June, that fertilize the ground for next year's flowers) has great Dharma meaning when we think deeply. Applying this broader perspective to everything we encounter helps us see others' behavior and our reactions to it as the result of numerous causes and current conditions. This cuts our inner dissatisfied, complaining dialogues, and replaces them with curiosity.

Looking at daily life in this way increases our understanding of dependent arising, the meaning of being conditioned phenomena, and karma and its effects.

135

Choosing to Stay Angry

~

Being angry doesn't mean we're bad people. We can't just tell ourselves, *I shouldn't be angry*, because *should* doesn't make any difference in reality. When we're angry, we're angry.

The choice is this: Do we want to continue to be angry and reap its consequences? Or do we want to apply the antidotes to anger and reap the benefits of returning to a balanced state of mind? That's the question before us when we're angry.

136

Happiness from Within

The misconception that external things and people can bring us ultimate happiness permeates our lives and leads to great disappointment. We're counting on things that simply don't have the ability to make us everlastingly happy. That doesn't mean there's no purpose in doing anything. We all know that there's enjoyment and that we can do good things in the world. The problem comes when we expect more of external things and people than they can really deliver.

When we engage in serious spiritual practice, we start to see that real joy and happiness come from transforming the mind. We're not so dependent on the outside world for our happiness, and in this way we become much freer. As a result, wherever we go, whatever we do, our happiness comes with us because our happiness comes from within, not outside.

137

Healing the Past

What happened in the past is not happening now.

Someone harmed you once, but every time you replay the situation in your mind your thoughts harm you all over again.

Instead you can say, "I need to make peace with the past and forgive what others did. I can have some compassion for them. Those people were just trying to be happy, but they were so confused and in so much internal pain. Look at what they did thinking they were going to bring happiness to themselves—they brought about the exact opposite and harmed me and others in the process."

Isn't that a situation that calls for compassion?

138

Our Most Important Task

The most important thing to do each day is to develop a kind heart. His Holiness the Dalai Lama points out that people of all faiths seek to cultivate a kind heart and compassion and to live ethically. People who aren't religious also support these goals because they know it makes society more peaceful and life more satisfying.

We each have a kind heart naturally, yet we must also work at developing it. I grew up hearing, "Love thy neighbor as thyself," which sounds great. However, I didn't know how to do this until I learned Buddhist thought-training techniques for developing a kind heart and forgiveness. The Buddha's instruction to reflect on the benefits of kindness and on how completely dependent we are on the kindness of others is also useful.

Some days we'll be successful with these methods, while other days we'll fall on our face. All we can do is pick ourselves up, try to relax our minds, and come back to developing a loving attitude. If we keep doing this, over time it will become second nature.

139

Our Time Together

~~~~~~~~

Every day, people are going out of or coming into our lives. Given that everything is impermanent and transitory, let's use our time together to generate compassion and wisdom, help one another on the path, support one another in our practice, and work for the benefit of sentient beings.

140

Contributing to World Peace

Any time we refrain from even one negative action, there's that much less negativity in the world. Since we're interdependent and we influence one another, when we refrain from harmful actions, those who would be the objects of those actions aren't harmed. Don't underestimate this, because just one person, such as Hitler or Stalin, can wreak havoc on many lives through their destructive actions.

Refraining from harmful actions is our individual contribution to world peace. People who meet us won't fear for their lives or property. Our presence allows them to feel secure, and they won't fear an angry outburst. All other ways of alleviating suffering must be based on abandoning actions motivated by the intention to cause others harm. In this way, our ethical conduct influences the people, animals, environment, and all of society around us in a positive way.

141

True Love

⁓

Love isn't like a song we hear on the radio: "I can't live without you and I'm going to die if you're not part of my life . . ." Such "love" is self-centered. The reality is that everyone else can live very well without them.

From a Dharma perspective, love is free of clinging. We want everyone to have happiness and its causes simply because they exist, not because they stroke our egos. Such unconditional love takes a long time to generate, but it is stable and free of the drama and manipulation of "if you really loved me you would . . ."

Worthy of Love and Compassion

Compassion is wanting someone to be free from suffering and its causes. Having compassion, we don't want to deliberately inflict pain on others out of anger or ignorance. Sure, we can bully people and make them afraid of us, but that doesn't alleviate our own suffering and it only brings suffering to others.

People often confuse fear with respect, thinking that when someone fears them it means that person respects them. In fact, fear and respect are totally different.

Instead of intimidating others or bossing them around, let's extend our love, wishing them to be happy. Everyone is worthy of love simply because they exist. And when others are happy, they don't harm us or others, so we're all better off.

143

Anger Is Useless

———

A journalist posed this question to His Holiness the Dalai Lama: "You were twenty-four when you fled your country and became a refugee. You haven't been able to return, and in the meantime you've witnessed genocide and the ecological devastation of your country. Yet you aren't angry at the Communist Chinese. Why?"

His Holiness replied, "If I were angry, I couldn't sleep well, I couldn't eat well, and I'd be totally miserable. What good would that do? It would benefit neither me nor the Tibetans."

The journalist stared at him in amazement.

144

Explode or Implode

~

We usually have two ways of dealing with our anger: we either explode and spew our anger onto the other person; or we implode, blame ourselves, and shut down.

For exploders, the solution is, "I'm right. You're wrong. You change!" We fight, insist on having the last word, and inflict as much damage as we can.

Imploders hold their anger in. Instead of yelling and throwing things, we shrink and back away. We close the door, sit in our room, and sulk.

Sometimes we go and talk to those who will reinforce our side of the story. That's a sneaky form of explosion, because our intention is to harm the other person by getting others on our side and against that person. Of course, while we're busy preparing for battle, the other person is out living their life.

We're the losers when we allow anger and vengeance to rule our minds.

145

We're Not Helpless

When we suffer, self-pity may be our choice emotion: *I'm helpless. I'm hopeless. Nothing goes well for me. Poor me (sniff).*

We may not be masters of the situation, but we're not helpless either. We have a moral responsibility to respond to suffering in a way that solves problems instead of creating more. By using thought-training techniques, we can transform adversity into the path to awakening. Compassion enables us to do this.

People who have suffered and have been healed by generating compassion can be of great benefit by becoming social activists or by engaging in social projects. Suffering can make us stronger and forces us to cultivate inner resources that we didn't know we had.

146

The Winds of Karma

Here we are, blown together by the winds of karma. It's not by accident, nor is it predestined. Due to causes and conditions, and specifically due to our previous actions, we find ourselves here.

The events in our lives and the feelings of pleasure and pain in response to them are conditioned. Sometimes we have happiness, other times misery, and often just neutral feelings. But from a Buddhist perspective, what happens to us is not as important as how we respond. How we respond to our experiences creates the causes for future happiness or suffering. Actions motivated by anger and greed create the causes for misery; actions springing from kindness and compassion create the causes for happiness.

How we respond is our choice.

147

Dealing with Illness

Illness and the suffering we experience as a result are caused not only by the immediate causes of infection by bacteria, viruses, and so forth, but also by our previous destructive actions. We may not know exactly what actions we did in previous lives, but we can get some idea by studying the texts that explain karma. This is what I did when suffering from hepatitis A in Nepal many years ago. The Buddhist perspective inspired me to make a strong determination not to engage in harmful actions. In addition, I stopped feeling sorry for myself and let go of my anger at the kitchen staff who didn't wash the vegetables well.

148

Releasing Fear and Anxiety Regarding Our Health

Often fear and anxiety about our health bring more suffering than the physical illness or injury itself. One way to release this anxiety is to generate compassion for those experiencing similar or even worse health difficulties by doing the taking-and-giving meditation. In this meditation, with compassion we imagine removing others' suffering and using it to destroy our own fears so that we can stop ruminating and worrying about ourselves. With love, we imagine our body, belongings, and merit becoming whatever others need. We offer it to them and imagine that they become healthy and relaxed. They then develop the aspiration to attain awakening, bodhicitta, and the wisdom realizing reality. This uplifts our mind and gives meaning to our life.

149

I Must Say Farewell

Wealth, friends and relatives, and our body are the three things we're most attached to. We are attached to our possessions and the success and comfort they represent. We cling to friends and relatives who give us appreciation and emotional security. We've never been separated from our body since birth and have spent our whole life taking care of it. At the time of death, these three remain here, while our consciousness goes on with all the karmic seeds we've planted through clinging.

Are we ready to say farewell to our possessions, dear ones, and body? If not, it is a helpful practice to imagine we are departing, and instead of experiencing angst and fear, to leave your attachments behind. Even better is to use our wealth to create merit while we are still alive, to pray to introduce our dear ones to the Dharma in future lives, and to gracefully exit this body, which is nothing more than recycled organic matter. Mentally rehearsing for death prepares us for this event that all of us will experience.

150

We Are Not Our Bodies

The more we base our identity on our body, the more we limit our potential. The more we base others' identities on their bodies, the more we tend to judge people according to the color of their skin, their age, their physical abilities, and their sex.

As practitioners who are aware of the pain of societal prejudice around physical differences and who want to develop universal love and compassion, we train ourselves to avoid categorizing people in this way. We seek to be able to look into each person's heart and see that everyone wants happiness and freedom from suffering.

Let's not imprison ourselves and others by judging and classifying them according to the appearance of their body.

151

The Meaning of Secluded Retreat

The great masters encourage us to live in a secluded place and retreat from the world. It is easy to misinterpret this and think we should live in a lone forest hut and not speak to anyone. While this is one form of seclusion that is appropriate at certain times, actual seclusion is to isolate your mind from ignorance, animosity, attachment, and self-centeredness.

When your mind is overwhelmed by afflictions, living in a secluded place for a period of time gives you the time and space to engage in deep practice. But by itself, living in a retreat setting won't purify your mind. In fact, it may make you more habituated to your bad habits because no one is around to point them out to you.

152

Mindfulness and Introspective Awareness

Mindfulness and introspective awareness are two mental factors that keep us on track. In terms of ethical conduct, mindfulness remembers our precepts, while introspective awareness checks our body, speech, and mind to see if we're abiding by them.

When meditating, mindfulness places the mind firmly on the meditation object so that it doesn't get distracted. Introspective awareness monitors the mind to make sure our attention remains on the object and doesn't wander to distraction, agitation, lethargy, or laxity. If our mindfulness is weak, introspective awareness notices that and calls up the antidotes to dispel the hindrances to concentration. Mindfulness then focuses on the meditation object again.

153

No Room for Despair

Sometimes we feel overwhelmed by helplessness in the face of the world's problems and injustices and fall into despair. There is no room for despair, however. The Buddhas and bodhisattvas are working hard to liberate sentient beings from cyclic existence and they need our help. Consider that they have been trying to lead us to awakening since beginningless time, but we resist engaging in the practice that will get us there. Even though we prefer to lie on the beach, watch a movie, or listen to our favorite music instead of attend Dharma classes or meditate, the Buddhas and bodhisattvas don't give up on us. Lifetime after lifetime, they endeavor to help us even though we progress at a snail's pace. Seeing the potential in us that we are blind to, they persevere in their efforts to help us.

Since they don't give up on us, how can we give up on ourselves or others?

154

Apologizing

~~~

When we recognize that we've acted inappropriately toward someone, we can purify our attitude, generate love and compassion toward them, and apologize. If possible, write or call them. If not, at least apologize mentally. Honestly admitting our bad attitude or behavior enables us to open our heart instead of defiantly clinging to the notion that we are right and they are wrong.

Apologizing lets others know that our mind has changed and it releases the bad energy between us and others. If the other person is hurt or angry, apologizing gives them the space to let go. Even if they don't, it relieves your mind from the pain of holding a grudge.

Apologizing is particularly important in families. It not only sets a good example for children, but also brings harmony to the whole family so that the children can grow up in an environment free from the tension of quarreling parents.

155

Forgiveness

~

Forgiveness means that we're going to stop being angry at the other person. It doesn't mean that what they did is okay, it simply means that we're going to stop torturing ourselves with anger and resentment.

Forgiving doesn't necessitate forgetting what happened. Some events, such as the Holocaust or slavery, should not be forgotten. We need to remember them to prevent reoccurrences of such tragedies. However, letting go of our anger enables us to heal and releases us from the self-created prison of hatred.

We can see a mistaken action and call it for what it is without being angry. We have the choice to respond in many different ways.

156

Confused Compassion

⁓

Sometimes compassion is confused with fixing others' problems. We can guide and influence others, but we can't fix their problems. Others must come to the understanding themselves that their present way of thinking or acting isn't bringing them happiness, and they have to want to change.

When someone confides in us, all they may need is empathic listening on our part. If we instead give them unasked for advice, they won't feel heard or understood. If we actively become involved in trying to fix them or their problem, it could disempower them. Sometimes "compassion" is actually a distraction from working on ourselves. We're so eager to prevent others' suffering that we don't look at our own suffering and neglect to purify our mind and develop our good qualities. The amount of good we can do for others is then vastly diminished.

It's important to understand what compassion is, how to develop it, and how to use it in a way that helps both ourselves and others.

157

Creating Opportunities for Others

Caring for the young is a natural biological instinct. We want a better future for them, and creating that future is part of our work to benefit others. But a better future won't come about simply by wishing for it or praying for it. If we want children to have opportunities to use their talents and abilities, we must create the conditions for that now; we must create those opportunities starting now.

Education is the key to developing the talents and abilities of children. Working to change systemic prejudice creates opportunities for children to contribute their knowledge and creativity to society. We must speak up and act now for this to come about. Benefiting others in this way is practicing the bodhisattvas' deeds.

158

Being Aware of the Opportunity to Connect

My friend had to go to the emergency room and was surprised by the kindness of the people there. It wasn't just that the staff provided services for her; it was the way they took special care of her and how they shared from their own lives that moved her so deeply.

Now when she walks down the street, she sees all strangers as equally kind, because she realizes that in a finger snap they could show her the same kindness as the people in the emergency room. Similarly, we may be strangers to others now, but an unexpected situation may come along that gives us an opportunity to be kind to them.

Slow down and be aware of the small opportunities to benefit others that arise in your daily life. You'll then have a chance to connect with others and help them feel secure, worthwhile, and appreciated. This will brighten your day, too.

159

Speaking Up to Benefit Others

Once my teacher asked me how one of his students was doing. I didn't think this person's actions were good, but didn't want to talk badly about them behind their back, especially to our teacher. I waffled, and my discomfort was apparent.

My teacher said sternly, "I need to know what's going on so that I can help that person. Without that knowledge, how can I help? If you speak truthfully without a spiteful motivation, that is not divisive speech."

That was a big lesson for me. We shouldn't let bad situations continue out of fear of looking like we're gossiping or creating disharmony. If our motivation is clear and we wish to benefit somebody, we need to communicate about their behavior to someone who is capable of helping them. This is one form of skillful speech.

160

Start Small

⁓

To be socially engaged, we must be practical. Thinking big gives us a long-term perspective, but when acting it's imperative to start small. If we bite off more than we can chew, there's a danger that we will later feel overwhelmed and become discouraged. But if we take small steps that are successful, we will be encouraged by the progress we see.

161

Stay Balanced

To benefit others, we must take care to maintain balance in our own lives. Pushing ourselves leaves us exhausted, and then instead of being able to benefit others, others must take care of us.

Holding unrealistic expectations is often the reason we push ourselves: we may want to accomplish an urgent matter that requires time to resolve, or we may see ourselves as the only ones who can remedy a problem when in fact others can help as well.

Maintaining time each morning and evening either for meditation or spiritual reading is essential to keep ourselves balanced and to prevent our positive motivation from deteriorating or ego's machinations from sabotaging our good work.

162

Three Kinds of Faith

In Buddhism, faith isn't blind belief or unquestioning acceptance. Buddhism speaks of three kinds of faith. With admiring faith, we hear about the qualities of the Three Jewels and admire them. With aspiring faith, we aim to cultivate and gain those qualities ourselves. Convictional faith arises from our understanding of the four teachings truths. This third type of faith is based on knowledge and investigation and is more stable than the first two.

Faith may also be understood as trust or confidence. It arises dependent on causes—specifically, through learning and contemplating the Dharma. Just telling ourselves to have faith doesn't give us faith. We must question and learn. Then our faith in the Three Jewels and our respect and gratitude for our spiritual mentors has a strong basis, brings joy to our minds, and inspires our practice.

163

Investigate the Teachings

⁓

Thinking for ourselves while learning from others is a balancing act. Our learning depends on others sharing their knowledge. Then we must think about and verify for ourselves what we have learned.

If our teachers tell us that we have a precious human life, do we believe simply because they said so? That won't bring stability to our practice. But if we think about the qualities of a precious human life and the great opportunities such a rebirth affords us, this will have a profound effect on our minds.

164

Seeking Advice

~

When we receive guidance from our spiritual mentors, we should try to understand the reasons behind their advice. That will help us follow their advice and benefit from it.

Some people go from one teacher to another, asking for advice on the same issue until someone tells them what they want to hear. This is not wise and wastes our teachers' precious time.

We should seek advice on topics related to the Dharma. Our teacher is not a lawyer, an investment broker, an engineer, or a family therapist. It is usually better to ask those professionals for advice on the matters on which they are experts.

It's fine to have different views than our teachers on social and political issues. We go to our teachers to learn the path to awakening, not to learn the virtues of butter tea—if there are any!

165

Respecting All Religions

All religions teach ethical discipline, generosity, kindness, love, and compassion. From a Buddhist viewpoint, it's good that there are many different religions because that enables everybody to follow the philosophy that suits them best. People have different dispositions and interests and are at different stages on the path, and the existence of multiple religions meets the variety of needs.

For centuries, beginning in ancient India, Buddhists and non-Buddhists have engaged in discussion and debate regarding their different philosophical views on the nature of reality. When this is done with mutual respect, it sharpens the intelligence of everyone involved.

166

A United Voice for Peace

~

In today's world, it is essential that all religious leaders speak with a common voice against violence, prejudice, exploitation, and injustice. Together we must advocate for human rights, cooperation, tolerance, diplomacy, equality, and peace.

While all religions share these values, how they define each may differ. We need to listen to one another from the heart regarding the practical issues of how we want to live our common values. When all religions show a united front against violence and discrimination, it is a powerful sight that opens people's minds and hearts.

167

Talking to Our Two-Year-Old Mind

Our two-year-old mind sports all kinds of dramas. It is resistant to meditation and puts forth many reasons why we can't meditate now, why attending Dharma class is inconvenient, and why it's impossible to go on retreat. The two-year-old pouts and has temper tantrums. It sulks and blames us for being the worst person alive, and then when its energy revives, it explodes in anger at the rest of the world who treats it unfairly. This is one reason why the scriptures refer to common beings as "childish" sentient beings.

When the two-year-old mind cries out, we can bring forth the adult mind that says with firmness and compassion, *I know you're upset, but it's important to learn to bear the frustration of not getting what you want.* The adult mind also kindly says, *I know you want to sleep more, but we're going to get up and meditate.*

168

Our Enemies Are Precious

~

We need to create a wealth of virtue to attain buddha-hood, and one of the best ways is by practicing forti-tude, the ability to remain calm in the face of suffering. We can't practice fortitude with people we like or those who are kind to us, so people we perceive as harming us are valuable for our Dharma practice. Why? Because to become a buddha, we need to complete the perfection of fortitude, and we can only practice that virtue with people we find disagreeable. In this respect, our enemies are like precious treasures who enable us to let go of our hostility and hurt and in their place develop love, com-passion, and tolerance.

Bodhisattvas rejoice when they encounter disagreeable people because it gives them the rare opportunity to prac-tice fortitude and compassion. Of course, being disagree-able, such people don't show up when bodhisattvas want them to. But that may have to do with bodhisattvas not seeing people as enemies.

169

The Lion of Pride

The Tibetan story about an intelligent rabbit who out-
witted an arrogant lion speaks to me. On the full moon,
the rabbit told the lion about a creature who was more
magnificent than the king of beasts. Astounded, the lion
wanted to confront this creature. The rabbit brought the
lion to a well and told him to look down. The lion began
to show off his strength. The being in the well did the
same. Then the lion growled, and the being in the well
returned the threat. Determined to defeat this creature,
the lion pounced on his own reflection in the water—and
drowned.

The best way to combat pride is to contemplate something we don't understand well. When we recognize that
we have limitations, our pride goes down. Another antidote to arrogance is to recognize that those we look down
on, compete with, or are jealous of have all been our parents and teachers in previous lives and have helped us
develop our talents. We didn't do it alone.

The Elephant of Ignorance

When ignorance is on a rampage, like a mad elephant, it creates all sorts of trouble. Ignorance of karma and its effects cannot discern between the causes of suffering and the causes of happiness, and therefore it takes us down the slippery slope of destructive actions. Ignorance of the ultimate nature of persons and phenomena apprehends people and things as existing in a way that is the complete opposite of how they actually exist. Ignorance believes phenomena that are dependent on other factors have their own independent essence. It gives rise to afflictions, which in turn keep us imprisoned in cyclic existence.

Wisdom is the elephant tamer that harnesses our out-of-control ignorance and directs the mind to the path of awakening. Wisdom regarding the functioning of cause and effect enables us to live ethically, thus creating the cause for fortunate rebirth. Understanding the ultimate nature of reality abolishes the self-grasping ignorance that prevents us from actualizing the bliss of awakening.

171

The Fire of Anger

—

When you're angry, does it feel like you're burning up?

Anger burns our good karma and produces negative karma. It quickly destroys harmony and trust, which are essential to have happy relationships. Like fiery lava, harsh words explode from our mouths. Like flowing lava, anger spreads everywhere, contaminating every aspect of our lives.

Training our minds in fortitude, the ability to remain calm in the face of harm or suffering, cools anger down. With fortitude, compassion and open-mindedness rule the mind, and we are able to clearly act—sometimes with peaceful strength, and other times with assertive compassion—in ways that benefit ourselves and others.

172

The Snake of Jealousy

⁓

When we're unable to bear others' wealth and good fortune, our mind becomes filled with poison. Trying to destroy their happiness, we lead ourselves to humiliation. It is difficult to respect ourselves when we have a heartless wish to inflict suffering on others.

Jealousy is really counterintuitive. We pray that others will have happiness and its causes, but when they do, our jealousy finds their talents, success, happiness, and good opportunities unendurable. With all the suffering in the world, why would we want to add to it, when all we need to do is open our hearts and let ourselves be happy about someone else's goodness and fortunate circumstances?

By rejoicing, we create merit without even lifting a finger. This way we easily join in others' happiness, which makes us feel good and others happy.

173

The Thieves of Wrong Views

Wrong views prevent us from finding the correct path to awakening. Like thieves, they steal our virtue and steer us in the wrong direction.

Due to wrong views, we fall to absolutism, we grasp ourselves and all phenomena as existing objectively, an independent reality "out there," when in fact everything is dependent and lacks its own inherent essence. Wrong views can also push us over the cliff into nihilism, believing that nothing exists at all, or that our actions lack any kind of moral dimension. These views destroy our respect for ethical conduct and make us heedless. They destroy our wisdom and merit and prevent us from realizing the truth.

Finding a qualified teacher and identifying the correct path are the ways to expel these thieves who steal our well-being. Studying, contemplating, and meditating on the Buddha's teachings enables us to evict and then lock the door behind these robbers so they can never return.

174

The Chains of Miserliness

~

Miserliness is a big liar. It weaves the story that the more we keep for ourselves, the more we'll have. It threatens us with poverty, saying that if we share with others we'll lose out. Miserliness doesn't believe the Buddha's teaching— that generosity brings wealth—and instead reinforces the anxiety of loss even when we're wealthy.

Miserliness keeps us chained to fear. It makes us hold on to things we haven't used in years—and may even have forgotten we have—out of the fear that if we give it away, we'll regret it. It prevents us from engaging in one of the easiest and most delightful activities of human beings: connecting with others through giving.

175

The Tsunami of Attachment

Imagine being caught in a tsunami. It tosses you about, slamming you against debris. Its power is overwhelming—you have no control, and you're exhausted from trying to stay above water to breathe. Unless you can grab onto something, you'll drown.

This is what attachment does to us. It keeps us helpless in cyclic existence, powerfully swept along by the currents of afflictions and karma, violently tossed by our clinging to our body, possessions, friends and relatives, and our very lives.

We need to grab hold of the life preserver that the Buddha offers, by reflecting on the transient nature of everything and everybody and the disadvantages of cyclic existence. Looking closely, we will see the impermanent and unsatisfactory nature of cyclic existence and the suffering that attachment to it brings to all sentient beings.

Safety is in sight.

176

The Carnivorous Demon of Doubt

~

The path goes this way, but we're not sure about following it. We doubt our ability to practice; we doubt the teachings and our teachers. We're not sure if the path we've been taught leads to where we want to go, or that the destination of awakening even exists. The carnivorous demon of doubt keeps us running in circles, unable to get off the roller coaster of cyclic existence that's making us sick. What do we do?

First, meditate on the breath to calm the mind. Then, slowly start to dismantle the doubt. Study the Buddha's teachings from a place of reasoning and clarity to find your motivation for practice, and reach accurate conclusions about the teachings. Let the light of the Buddha's teachings dispel the darkness of doubt, and enjoy what you now see and understand.

You are capable, the path works, and awakening is possible!

177

Dependently Arising Appearances

Things, people, and events aren't as real as they appear to our senses. They are dependently arising appearances— dependent on the causes and conditions that create them, the parts that compose them, and the mind that conceives and designates them.

We may experience these appearances as pleasant or unpleasant. This too depends on circumstances and karma. But when we grasp these appearances to be real, the mind proliferates with attachment, anger, jealousy, and arrogance, and thus begins our struggle in the world.

This entire confused scenario that brings us suffering depends on the mind, which is the creator of our experiences.

Understanding dependent arising leads to developing the wisdom that realizes the emptiness or lack of independent existence. This wisdom liberates us from cyclic existence.

178

Inconceivable Interdependence

⁓

Sometimes I think about the person who in 1975 posted a flyer about a meditation course at the Bodhi Tree Bookstore in Los Angeles. Thanks to this one small action, I became involved in the Dharma, and life turned out very different than it would have been otherwise. Meanwhile, other events that I thought would have a tremendous impact on my life never did.

As ordinary beings, we know so little about the specific conditions that cause our lives to unfold in one way or another. Everything exists interdependently, and we can't always see the full picture of all the factors at play. However, one thing is for sure: if we create virtuous causes and don't destroy them by anger or wrong views, happiness will definitely come.

179

Only This Life

~

When disturbing emotions arise strongly in relation to certain words or events, it's helpful to tell yourself, *This is just an event of this life. I don't need to react with such intensity to it; it will quickly change.* After all, in countless previous lives you've gotten very upset and overwhelmed by strong emotions, but right now you don't remember any of those situations. Only the karmic seeds of your responses to those situations remain, and these will influence your future experiences.

Bringing that understanding into the present, see that it's not helpful to make a big deal about what happens to you now—you won't remember it later anyway. It's more useful to be attentive to your responses because those will affect you later in this life or in some future life. Let the mind relax, view the situation from a more realistic perspective, and then respond to it with compassion.

180

Our Purpose in Life

~

If the purpose of our life is simply to keep the body alive, to eat, sleep, and experience pleasure, then at the end of our life we'll have nothing to show for it. The body will die and all our pleasures will disappear like last night's dreams.

But if we work with a broader motivation, doing what benefits living beings and working for a long-term noble purpose, then we'll feel good about ourselves now and will experience happiness in the future. At the end of our life we'll be at peace with ourselves, and the seeds of virtuous karma will go with our mindstream into the next life. In addition, the benefit we gave others will have a ripple effect, spreading far and wide through the actions of those we benefitted.

181

Attachment Is a Pain in the Neck

People tend to judge themselves harshly, for example, thinking that they are bad because they are attached to sense pleasures, possessions, or people.

Judging ourselves is senseless. The point is to see that attachment causes us misery and is antithetical to our deepest spiritual aspirations. This can be seen by looking at our own experiences: see how attachment makes us dissatisfied so that we long for what we don't have or are discontent with what we do have. Watch how attachment makes us lie to get what we want, pretend to have qualities we don't have, or deceive others into believing we don't have the negative attributes that we do have.

A deeper understanding of how attachment functions makes us more willing to give it up; relinquishing attachment and craving allows us to be peaceful and gives us an opportunity to use our time in more satisfying ways.

182

Letting Go of Unhappiness

Instead of blaming people or things outside of ourselves when we're unhappy, look inside and ask, *What thoughts are making me unhappy?* and *What am I holding onto that's making me unhappy?*

Sometimes we think, *I must always be comfortable*, or *Everyone must like me*, or *I am always right*, or *I must win this argument at all costs*. Such thoughts trap us in misery.

When you are troubled, try to identify and release whatever false thoughts are the source of your unhappiness.

183

Clear Communication

One way to express compassion is to be as clear as possible in our communication. Sometimes this is difficult because we aren't clear ourselves about what we think or want to express, even though we think we may be. Only later do we realize our own confusion.

When we aren't clear in our own minds, it's best to say that directly and tell the other person and let them know we need more time to clarify our ideas.

When I'm tangled up, I've found it helpful to stop, let go of all the thoughts and ideas, and simply ask myself, *What am I trying to say?* That helps me get to the heart of the matter, the one sentence that is the essence of what I want to communicate.

184

Accepting Apologies

⁓

Accepting apologies from others is part of our practice of generosity and fortitude. After others apologize, if we still hold a grudge and want to retaliate, then anger is running the show and causing us suffering.

Their apology doesn't mean we gloat over the thought that we were right. Rather, their apology indicates that they have grown and are brave enough to take responsibility for the harm they caused. Their apology also lets us know that they acknowledge our suffering. Gracefully accepting another's apology is an expression of compassion and a way to heal.

185

Listening in Conflicts

———

When a friend vents their anger at another person to us, listening with understanding and without judgment is a great gift. Although it may seem that they want us to take their side against the other party, our doing so won't help and only gets us involved in something that isn't any of our business.

When our friend rattles off a litany of the other person's perceived transgressions, we can respond, "It sounds like you're angry. Are you needing respect? Do you need a say in what is happening?"

We can guess at what our friend may be feeling and needing, and give them space to discuss this without referencing it to the other person. We can then talk about ways to see the situation differently so that anger evaporates.

This is a wise way to support a friend.

186

The Willingness to Face Suffering

Pain is part of having a body and mind under the influence of afflictions and karma. It happens to all of us. Instead of fearing pain or suffering, we can face it with wisdom that accepts the situation. Wisdom can also be derived from suffering experiences: suffering leads us to investigate our situation of being in cyclic existence. What is it? What causes it? Is it possible to stop it, and if so, what is the path to doing that?

There are other benefits to accepting suffering: pain attunes us to others' experiences and increases our compassion. It deflates our arrogance and reminds us we are fallible human beings just like others.

Recalling that all our experiences are impermanent assures us that unpleasant experiences depend on causes and conditions and that they will end. Engaging in the taking-and-giving meditation draws our attention away from our own pain and broadens our view. In this meditation, we imagine taking on others' pain with compassion and with love giving them everything they need in this life and beyond.

187

A Quiet Place

Have you ever had the experience of going outside and suddenly the silence strikes you because it's in such sharp contrast with the chatter in your mind? The external silence brings relief from the internal commotion.

Since a quiet environment isn't always nearby, we can learn to get in touch with the quiet place in our own hearts—that peaceful place that accepts what is happening at present, knows that it will change, and understands that we can change in the future. This is the quiet place inside us that can smile at the world with humor and kindness.

We want to learn to notice that chatter before we even walk outside. We want to be able to find that quiet place inside ourselves and keep it with us, so that even when we're in a noisy environment the mind can be quiet.

188

Are Buddhists Pessimistic?

~

Reflecting on the disadvantages of cyclic existence makes us realistic, not pessimistic. We accurately see what cyclic existence is and what it isn't. In the process, our enchantment with cyclic existence diminishes and we let go of the fantasy that we'll find ultimate security and bliss in cyclic existence.

This allows us to deal with cyclic existence in a practical and realistic way, without whitewashing its defects or projecting magnificence that isn't there. It doesn't mean that we assume the worst is going to happen; that, too, is unrealistic. Rather, we have more realistic expectations and learn how to transform adversity into the path by changing our perspective.

189

Baby Bodhisattvas

⌒

Having a positive vision of what we can become is important for everyone. Unfortunately, in communities where children see poverty, gun violence, and so on, this is the vision they have of their future. Not seeing a possible alternative, they replicate the behavior of their older siblings and parents, bringing the same tragic results.

The need for a positive image of what we can become spiritually is essential. The Buddha; Chenrezig, the manifestation of compassion; and Tara, the female manifestation of awakening become our role models. Perhaps we can't relate to having a body made of light and having equal compassion for all sentient beings right now, but we can see that each of us has the seeds of compassion and wisdom within us. The small beginnings of the buddhas we will eventually become exist in us now.

Let's generate the intention to nourish these seeds and act so that these seeds will sprout, grow, and flourish.

190

Our View of Impermanence

From one perspective, impermanence can be seen as a cause of suffering—everything we cherish disintegrates, and whatever comes together will separate. Understanding this inspires us to seek liberation from cyclic existence.

From another perspective, impermanence can be seen as positive: the fact that our anger and afflictions don't always manifest in our minds is a relief. The fact that all our good qualities can grow limitlessly is a source of optimism.

We must hold both perspectives and focus on one or the other according to what is needed to keep our minds balanced at any given moment.

191

How to Rest

The common notion of rest usually involves sleeping and lying around. If you think that monitoring your physical, verbal, and mental actions is stressful, you might let go of mindfulness and introspective awareness in order to "rest." But letting the mind wander to whatever object it wants to attach to isn't rest—it's distraction and often only increases one's stress.

Real rest is resting in emptiness, the nature of reality, the emptiness of inherent existence. Focusing on the ultimate mode of existence—the lack of all the fantasized modes of existence that ignorance has projected on people and things—is a wondrous rest. When the mind rests in emptiness, ignorance, attachment, and anger cannot manifest.

Real rest also involves resting the mind in bodhicitta. When we do that, there's no partiality or prejudice; the critical judgment mind relaxes. Resting the mind from the barrage of afflictions is actual peace.

192

A Good Relationship with Our Body

Motivated by attachment, we create so much destructive karma in our efforts to protect and please this body. We kill and steal to protect this body. We participate in unwise and unkind sexual relationships to give it pleasure. We lie, talk behind others' backs, and speak harshly, all to give this body pleasure and protect it from harm.

At the end of our life, the body becomes a rotting corpse that nobody wants to go near. Our consciousness goes on to the next life with all the karmic seeds we have created as a result of our actions and our attachment to our body.

A good relationship with our body involves keeping it clean and healthy so that we can use it to practice the path to awakening. We accept the body without being a slave to its wants.

193

A Weapon of Mass Destruction

~

Although we may not be able to control the weapons of mass destruction proliferating in the world, there is one that we can control—our own speech.

If we lack mindfulness, our speech can create massive damage for many living beings. Four nonvirtues of speech—lying, disharmonious words, harsh speech, and idle talk—can tear apart relationships, break the trust that has been built over a long time, create tremendous confusion and anxiety, and deceive other people so that they make decisions that bring devastation to themselves and others.

Speech includes all forms of communication—verbal, written, and body language. None of us can afford to dismiss the effect of our speech on those around us and on the world as a whole.

194

Little (and Big) Lies

—

Whenever you think that you must lie, it's good to ask yourself, *What am I doing that I don't want others to know about?*

If you lie to cover up your actions, what you're doing is usually not such a good thing to start with. For example, if you're having an affair and lying to your spouse about it, you must ask yourself why you're having an affair and what you can do to improve your relationship with your spouse.

You may justify little white lies by saying you don't want to hurt others' feelings, but actually this motivation is self-centered—it's used to protect your reputation or to get what you want.

195

Speaking the Truth

When you speak the truth and act on the basis of truth, others will trust you. Even though events may not turn out in your favor from a worldly perspective, in the long run you'll experience a result based on the truth.

Speaking the truth involves not intentionally being deceptive as well as not being harmful. To tell a hunter where the deer went is not speaking the truth—it will harm the deer and bring suffering to the hunter in the long run, since he is putting the seed of destructive karma on his mindstream.

196

The Truth in Business

~

Every year the same businessman asks me, "How can I do business without lying? It's impossible!"

I tell him about a friend who worked at a large corporation in Hong Kong. She told me that if you lie and deceive clients and customers, you may reap some immediate benefit, but eventually they will realize that you have cheated them and will never work with you again. In addition, instead of recommending your company to others, they will tell people that your company is untrustworthy and you will end up with a bad reputation.

As we were told when we were children, "Honesty is the best policy."

197

Harmony or Disharmony

Motivated by jealousy or resentment, we may seek to cause people who are harmonious to quarrel. Or we may spread rumors in our workplace and encourage our colleagues to join us in scapegoating another colleague. Creating factions in an organization, a community, or a family may give us a perverse delight. But what good do all these activities do?

Whenever someone speaks badly about another person to me, I distance myself from that person. If they criticize somebody behind that person's back to me, I know they will criticize me behind my back to others.

198

Shaming or Encouraging

Harsh speech so easily comes out of our mouths when we are in a bad mood. We may also send a scathing email or text to someone when we are frustrated. The other person may not have even done anything particularly disturbing, but we scold and insult them over a small matter.

Adults sometimes take perverse pleasure in ridiculing or teasing children, or even making them afraid by telling them the boogeyman will get them. Other times we try to bolster our own self-esteem by humiliating or shaming others. Of course, it doesn't work.

Rather, we should use our speech to point out others' good qualities and positive actions, which gladdens our hearts as well as theirs.

199

Saying What We Vowed Never to Say

Many new parents tell me that they find the very same words coming out of their mouths that their parents said to them—words they vowed never to say to their children, words of blame, humiliation, and shame.

This is due to our habitual tendencies to think and speak in that way. We must break the habit of venting our frustration on children. We know from our own experience how detrimental harsh words are to young children, who then think they are inferior or not worthwhile human beings.

Sometimes Mom and Dad need to say, "I need a time out," and go to another room to calm themselves by taking slow, deep breaths. Then they can return, listen to the children's frustration, and show the children the kind of behavior that they would like from them.

200

People Are like Pianos

If we take our time and learn to play the piano, we'll hear a beautiful melody. But if we just bang the keys, we all know what that sounds like.

There was a person who disturbed me no end with her constant complaining. Telling her to cut it out didn't help at all. But when I complimented her on her beautiful flower arrangements, she beamed. When I shared my appreciation for the invitation to her birthday party, she again softened. I learned that if I commented on her good qualities, we got along much better. She became like a piano with delightful tunes.

201

Blah, Blah, Blah

~

The fourth kind of speech to watch out for is idle talk—spending hours talking about topics that have no real value. It's done for amusement or to make ourselves look important in some way. This not only takes up other people's precious time, but also wastes our own time.

This doesn't mean that all our conversations must be deep and meaningful. To have harmonious relationships with friends, colleagues, and family, we may chitchat for a bit, but we should be aware of what we're saying and why. We should steer away from gossip and topics that provoke attachment or envy in both ourselves and others, and make an effort to draw out others and learn about them as human beings.

202

Idle Talk

—

Discerning the difference between idle talk and appropriate talk is not always straightforward. Sometimes we might talk about politics or a television movie for a specific purpose. We're aware of what we're doing, and our motivation is sensible. This isn't idle talk.

Other times we may talk about something meaningful, even the Dharma, but just want to hear ourselves talk, to hang out, or to do something with our restless energy. The topic may seem beneficial, but our motivation is one of idle talk.

Developing skillful speech involves repeatedly observing our speech, our motivation for speaking, and the situation. Through this process we learn to discern what is appropriate or inappropriate to speak about, which people to speak to, and when to do so.

203

The Story of Our Guilt

~~~

There's a big difference between regretting our mistakes and feeling guilty.

Regret is: "I made a mistake. I'm going to learn from it and move on."

Guilt says: "How could I have done that? I'm so terrible. I can't face the world again. It's all my fault."

Why do we feel so much guilt? For some of us, it's what was instilled in us as kids. The nice thing about being an adult is that we can examine what we were taught when we were young to see if it makes sense or not. When we do so, it's evident that guilt is rubbish.

Sit down and write out what the guilty mind is telling you and ask yourself, *Is that true?* Then put the guilt down and ask, *Have I done things that I regret?* If so, acknowledge them, make amends, and learn from those mistakes.

204

Many Shades of Pride

Most forms of pride involve feeling superior and wanting others to recognize our special qualities. However, there is another type of pride—the pride of inferiority that thinks we're special because we're worse than everyone else. There's also the pride of association: we consider ourselves great because we know someone who's important. Then there's simply the pride of "I am"—the arrogance of existing that grasps an independent person who is the master of their body and mind and who thinks they should be able to control others as well.

The ultimate antidote to pride is meditation on emptiness, which examines how the "I" exists, only to discover that this seemingly important self cannot be found. The self changes in every moment and lacks essence. It is not our body; it is not our mind; and it is not something other than our body and mind. It exists by being merely designated.

Other antidotes to pride include reflecting on its disadvantages or the fact that all the qualities we pride ourselves on depend on others who taught and encouraged us. Contemplating our precious human life and our buddha-nature is the antidote to the pride of inferiority. Apply whichever antidote works best for the type of pride.

205

Bowing

⁓

Bowing is an ancient Buddhist custom, one found in nearly all religions. If we don't understand the purpose of bowing and the beneficial effect it has on our mind, we may balk at it.

We bow to the Three Jewels to show respect to their excellent qualities and to open ourselves to cultivating those same qualities. We respect and emulate the Buddha, the Dharma, and the Sangha, taking them as our spiritual refuge and guides. We bow to other practitioners whom we respect and who are good role models for us.

Bowing is also a way of acknowledging the buddha-nature and goodness in each person we encounter. By creating an attitude of humility and respect in our minds, bowing softens our tendency to pick at others' faults and enables us to give them feedback in a way that they can more easily accept.

206

Protecting Our Merit

—

Dedicating the merit we create through generosity, ethical conduct, and other virtuous actions steers it so it will ripen in the results we seek. When we dedicate for the highest, long-term goal of full awakening, our merit will not be exhausted until that occurs, and in the meantime it will ripen in a series of fortunate rebirths so that we can continue to practice the path. If we dedicate only for a good rebirth or only for happiness in this life, these will come if other conditions allow, but after the merit ripens it will be finished.

Compassionately dedicating for the well-being and awakening of all sentient beings enhances our merit. Dedicating with an awareness of dependent arising—that everything exists dependent on other things and nothing exists independently—strengthens our merit and makes it powerful. This involves reflecting on the idea that because the merit, the awakening we dedicate it for, and ourselves as the ones who are dedicating all exist dependently, they are empty of any inherent existence.

Merit can be dedicated silently, or we can chant a verse such as, "Due to this merit, may I soon attain the state of guru Buddha, so that I may be able to liberate all sentient beings from their suffering."

207

Commitment to Kindness

Every morning, reaffirm your commitment to kindness. Because negative emotions—especially confusion, greed, and animosity—are powerful and our mind is easily swept up by them, it's important to again and again remind ourselves of kindness. It's essential on a regular basis to think of the values and principles that we cherish—such as fairness, equality, generosity, forgiveness, compassion, care, and kindness—and to commit to them repeatedly.

Even when things aren't going the way we want, even when there are problems everywhere, come back to regarding the world and its inhabitants with kindness and to treating ourselves and others with kindness.

208

Transforming Painful Situations

⁓

Sometimes, letting go of pain takes a long time. We may have seen or experienced a traumatic event. We may have been treated unfairly. We may be disappointed in our own bad behavior that has harmed others.

When painful thoughts of the past arise, imagine the Buddha is there with you. Imagine that you respond as the Buddha would, with wisdom and compassion. Imagine that compassionate light emanates from the Buddha and fills everyone in the scene—both those who inflicted harm and those who experienced harm—and think that all of them relax and release their pain and suffering.

As the light of the Buddha continues to flow into them, imagine their minds opening and that they each make the decision to abandon harm and to benefit others. Rest your mind in that.

209

Interrupt the Interrupting

~

Listening from the heart is a skill that benefits ourselves and others. Several factors are involved:

First, we must respect others and genuinely want to learn from them and connect to them.

Second, we must refrain from interrupting. In many occasions listening is more important than speaking. Even though I may have what I consider a brilliant idea or the perfect retort, I tell myself, *You'll have a chance to speak later—listen now.*

Third, we must refrain from telling people they shouldn't feel what they're feeling. We don't need to agree with their feelings, but putting someone down for feeling what they're feeling usually makes them withdraw from the conversation. This, in addition to humiliating, ridiculing, or not giving others an adequate chance to express themselves, stops communication in its tracks. We may "win" the conversation, but if others feel resentful and don't trust us afterward, have actually lost.

210

Clinging to the Impossible

When we hear that a good friend or relative is dying or we think about our own death, it seems that there's a real, solid person that will soon be gone. When we examine this idea, however, we find that there's no solid person there to start with. There's just a body and a mind. The body is not the person, the mind is not the person, the collection of the two isn't the person, and there's no person apart from them. The self exists because on the basis of the body and mind we conceive and designate a "person." Forgetting that we designated the person, we believe there's a real person there. Grasping at this erroneous idea of the person, we fear losing them.

Yet always being together is impossible. Whatever comes together must separate. Causes and conditions control our lives; there is not a self-sufficient person in charge, even though our ignorance thinks there is.

The real tragedy of the ignorant mind is that it holds on to things that are impossible to keep. This refusal to accept the true nature of reality brings so much suffering.

How to Watch the News

Watching the news is a live teaching on karma and its effects. We see people experiencing the results of previously created constructive and destructive actions, as well as people creating the causes of either future happiness or suffering. Care is needed not to judge anyone—not to disparage those who are suffering due to their past actions, and not to think that those who experience happiness now are morally superior. Similarly, let's not rejoice that people who act in harmful ways will suffer in the future or think that those creating virtue today are morally above everyone else.

No one deserves to suffer, and no divine being is rewarding or punishing us. We experience the results of the actions that we ourselves do. Let's use our understanding of karma to generate compassion for everybody involved, because everyone is trying to be happy, and everyone creates the causes of their own misery due to ignorance. Let's extend our compassion to everyone we see on the news, no matter what they are experiencing or doing.

212

It's All about Me

I once received a request from *Self* magazine to reprint something that I had written. It was a magazine for women, and their website at that time said their premise was to let women know that "it's all about me."

I thought, *I've spent years training my mind to see that it's not all about me. There's only one of me and billions of others. Thinking it's all about me is just suffering.*

Our society promotes this idea that it's all about me, and the self-centered mind loves it. Practicing the Dharma means we've got to swim upstream and go against not only what society tells us, but also what the ego enjoys. The fact is, it's all about all sentient beings. Cherishing them is the key to our own happiness and awakening.

213

Is It Happening Now?

—

You're meditating in a quiet, safe place, and suddenly you remember the harsh insults someone threw at you ten years ago. Hurt feelings arise, anger flares, thoughts of revenge burn.

Time goes by, the bell rings. You open your eyes and the horrible scene that was just tormenting you is nowhere to be seen. It was all conceptual thought; it's not happening now, it was all made up by the mind.

Return to the present and recall that the person insulted you once, but every time you recall the incident with anger, you insult yourself again. Resolve that the next time harmful situations from the past arise, you'll press the "pause" button and think, *This is not happening now. I don't want to die ruminating on a past harm, so why let my mind do it now?*

214

Digging Ourselves into a Hole

⁓

Sometimes we dig ourselves into a nice, deep hole with our bitter, angry way of thinking. We sit in the hole and moan, "The world's falling apart, it's all useless."

We decorate the hole and make ourselves as comfortable as possible, even though thorns and shards jab us. We keep curling up, making this hole our home, even to the point of becoming upset if someone suggests there are more comfortable places we could live.

All we need to do is stop and say, "There's a remedy to this situation. There are many people who can throw me a rope if I bothered to ask them."

With time and practice, it will become easier to detect when we're digging a hole for ourselves and stop the excavation. Sitting in the sunshine feels much better.

215

The Feel-Good Four Immeasurables

As part of our daily practice, we may recite the four immeasurables:

May all sentient beings have happiness and its causes. *(Oh, wonderful!)*

May all sentient beings be free of suffering and its causes. *(Very wonderful!)*

May all sentient beings not be separated from sorrowless bliss. *(Oh, I'm floating on a cloud!)*

May all sentient beings abide in equanimity, free of bias, attachment, and anger. *(What a wonderful, ideal world!)*

We feel great, but when we come out of meditation . . .

"Somebody left a mess in the living room. Who do they think they are? This is totally unacceptable, I must confront him!" Our feel-good four immeasurables are out the window. We don't catch our anger or see our lack of equanimity, let alone our love, compassion, and joy. The feel-good aspect and the reality of our mind are worlds apart.

Back to the meditation cushion to try again, this time trying to integrate these four thoughts into our own minds.

216

Equanimity: Why Do I Feel the Way I Do?

To generate bodhicitta, equanimity is the foundation. Equanimity is a mental state that is free from attachment to friends, animosity toward enemies (people we don't like or feel antipathy toward), and apathy toward strangers.

Think of a friend and ask yourself, *Why am I attached to them?* Then think of someone you don't like and ask yourself, *Why do I feel animosity toward enemies?* Finally, imagine a stranger and ask yourself, *Why do I feel apathy toward strangers?*

There are no right or wrong answers—and don't try to pretend that you don't have these thoughts. What word did you hear in all three of your responses?

That's right, *me.* Hmm, what does that mean?

217

Equanimity: Categorizing People

We believe that friends are inherently wonderful people from their own side, so of course it's natural to be attached to them. Similarly, enemies are inherently obnoxious from their own side, so we're justified in feeling repelled and hostile toward them. And strangers, it's only natural to be apathetic, isn't it? After all, there are just too many people to care about all of them.

When we look closer, we discover that people aren't friends, enemies, or strangers from their own side, but because we put them in those boxes. People who are nice to me, understand me, give me gifts, help me accomplish projects, and so forth are deemed friends, and so we become attached to them. We see people who interfere with our happiness as enemies and are hostile toward them. And since we don't know strangers, why have any feelings at all toward them?

In short, we create friends, enemies, and strangers by judging people in terms of how they treat *me*.

218

Equanimity: Caring for Everyone Equally

~~~

Seeing the self-centered fallacy of how we judge people, let's put it aside and recognize that the roles people play in our lives change all the time.

Sue gives us a gift today, and we say she's a friend; Pete criticizes us, and we regard him as an enemy. The next day Sue criticizes us and Pete gives us a gift, and the way we see them changes. No one is inherently a friend, enemy, or stranger. No one is always in one camp or another.

It's much more reasonable and realistic to care for all beings equally. After all, everyone equally wants happiness and not suffering. And everyone throughout beginningless time has been a friend, an enemy, and a stranger to us.

219

Hoping I'm Wrong

It happens that everyone in a group I'm working with favors a plan that I don't think will work well. I voice my concerns, but they don't resonate with the others. So unless I vehemently disagree, I go along with the group's decision and think, *I hope I'm wrong and that their idea works.* Rather than try to sabotage their plans for the strange "pleasure" of saying, "I told you so," I try to help them out. Lo and behold, their plan works well, and we all share in the happy result.

220

Creating Trust

⁓

In addition to speaking the truth, respecting others' property is necessary to create trust. This entails asking others before we use their things, treating their belongings with care, and returning what we borrow in a timely manner.

Being reliable and responsible is another way we can create trust. When we say we'll do something, we do it, and if something comes up where we can't, we let the other person know in advance so that they will not be inconvenienced in the case of small things, or feel that their trust has been betrayed in the case of major events.

All these small things in daily life are actually quite important when it comes to developing and maintaining trust and affection among people and living a happy life.

221

Stretching Our Boundaries

We tend to stay around the people we already know, people who are like us and who understand us. But in many ways this limits our growth and may contribute to arrogance and to isolating ourselves from others who are different.

At a large, month-long program with diverse participants, I gave myself the homework assignment of having a meaningful discussion with each and every person there. I would reach out and find common ground with people I perceived as being very different from me—different interests, different backgrounds, and so forth. What a wonderful and expanding experience this was! I learned that if I try, I could have a good discussion with anyone. In addition, many of my assumptions and stereotypes were proven wrong.

222

I'm Not a Thief

⁓

We usually think of stealing as akin to armed robbery and think, *I'd never do that!* But do we take things that haven't been freely offered to us? That is the meaning of stealing.

For example, do we take things at our workplace for personal use? Do we return money and belongings we've borrowed, or do we "forget" and consider them ours? Do we replace things that we borrowed and broke? Do we avoid paying taxes and fees that we're supposed to pay? Do we clock in and get paid for hours we didn't work?

Contemplating these questions will increase our mindfulness and introspective awareness. Straightening up our relationship with others' belongings will protect us from the destructive karma of taking what has not been freely given.

223

Hinting

~

The Buddha's teaching on the five wrong livelihoods details five deceptive ways that we use to get what we want: hinting, flattery, giving a small gift to get a big one, putting someone in an awkward position, and hypocrisy. Although this teaching principally applies to the ways monastics should not procure their requisites of food, clothing, shelter, and medicine, it also applies to the rest of us. What's startling is that I was taught as a child that asking directly for what we want was impolite, while a couple of these five were the polite way to let someone know you wanted them to give you something.

Avoiding hinting is a challenge. I dare not say what I really mean, which is "give me that," but instead couch it in concealed terms: "The jacket you gave me last year was so warm and comfortable. But it's old now and I'm not sure how to get one that is of the same high quality as the one you gave me last year."

224

Flattery

———

Because we are embarrassed by our greed or we fear that speaking in a straightforward manner is impolite, we may flatter someone with the hidden intention of getting what we want: "You're so generous. I really respect and rejoice at how openhearted you are and how willing you are to share what you have. Very few people are as unselfish as you are."

Of course, if we really mean that and say it without any intention of flattering the person, it's fine. But if our motivation is crooked, our flattering words are essentially lies. When the other person discovers our insincerity, they will no longer trust what we say. Is getting a little money or a gift worth this?

225

Giving a Small Gift to Get a Big One

Instead of getting in touch with our generous heart, we connive, thinking, *This person will like me if I give them a gift. The gift can be inexpensive, but if I wrap it nicely and add a card, they'll be so pleased they'll want to give me a gift in return. Since they've got more money than me, they'll give me something really nice.*

This is not generosity; it's the way "polite" people bribe one another. Seen this way, I don't think most of us would want to contribute to normalizing such behavior.

226

Putting Someone in an Awkward Position

⁓

Even when we're fundraising for a good cause, it's better not to put someone in an awkward position by saying, for example, "Ten people have given a hundred dollars and ten more have donated two-hundred fifty dollars. Now, how much would you like to give? Any amount is fine." Most people would feel embarrassed to say that they weren't interested in giving or that they didn't have enough money to give. They would feel pressured, especially if other people gave a lot.

It's much better to talk with someone about how their gift will be used and the benefit it will bring to others so that they feel inspired and joyous to contribute, even if they can only afford a small donation.

227

Who Me, a Hypocrite?

There's a Tibetan story about a monk in retreat who, wanting to impress his benefactor who was coming to visit that day, made elaborate offerings on his altar. He set out his tantric implements and a thick Dharma text, making it look like he was a serious and accomplished adept. Later he realized his hypocrisy and threw dirt on his altar before his benefactor arrived. His teacher, who saw all of this with his clairvoyant powers, commented, "Throwing that dirt was the best offering he made."

Being genuine counts more than fake appearances.

228

"Not Sure, Not Sure"

~~~

When our mind gets stuck in a tense situation, it's good to remember that whatever we are worried about or dreading is not sure to happen. As His Holiness the Dalai Lama says, "We don't know what the future will be until it happens."

Similarly, when we're excited about something positive, it's good to remember that it too is not a sure thing, and so to avoid getting too stirred up and inflated with fantastic expectations.

When we take good circumstances for granted, it's good to remember "not sure, not sure," which wakes us up from complacency. We remember to use our time wisely while we have good health and our mind is functioning well.

"Not sure" also opens us up to smiling at whatever life brings.

229

Dharma or Sense Pleasures?

The foundation of our spiritual practice is renunciation, the mind that wants to be free of suffering and unsatisfactoriness in all its forms—not just the "ouch" kind of suffering, but the whole situation of having a body and mind under the control of ignorance, afflictions, and karma. Otherwise, Dharma is just a hobby.

Unfortunately, when we face a choice between the Dharma and sense pleasures, we usually opt for sense pleasures—not just those pleasures that are the result of seeing, hearing, and so forth, but the whole emotional gooeyness of sticky relationships.

We need to repeatedly contemplate: What happens when our minds are constantly drawn to sense pleasures? What happens to our ethical discipline, our wish to benefit others, our love, compassion, and wisdom? All these get compromised.

230

Buddhism Exists within Culture

—

The Dharma—the true path that knows reality as it is and the cessation of suffering that results from it—is beyond culture. The Dharma can liberate the minds of all people, no matter their culture, ethnicity, race, sexual orientation, gender, and so forth. The true Dharma cannot and must not be altered according to culture.

The external appearance of the Dharma, however, adapts to each culture. In Tibet, vast open areas meet the eye, so the temples are full of statues, paintings, banners, and other colorful objects. In Southeast Asia, the landscape is green and colorful, so the altars in temples are uncluttered. In Southeast Asia and Tibet, robes are various shades of saffron. In China, historically only the emperor could wear that color, so the Sangha usually wears what is considered to be bland colors: black, gray, and brown. There is no absolute good or bad regarding such things.

231

Gender Equality

~

In ancient times, women were seen as weaker because their physical strength lay not in winning a physical battle but in giving birth. In ancient India, women were under the protection and control of first their fathers, then their husbands, and finally their sons.

These views are culturally bound and no longer pertain. The Buddha challenged them even in his time. He was radical because he established the order of fully ordained nuns and declared that women could attain liberation.

Nowadays, ancient views of the roles of both men and women no longer hold, and people seek equality between the sexes and equal opportunity for women in all areas of life. If Buddhism is going to continue to spread in Western cultures, Buddhist institutions must embody gender equality. It would be a great loss if we held on to outmoded views that make both men and women turn away from the Dharma.

232

The Dharma Relates to All Aspects of Our Lives

Dharma practice isn't something we do just while sitting on the cushion or only on Sunday mornings. It pertains to all aspects of our lives. Dharma influences how we treat family members, colleagues, friends, and strangers. It should influence our views on social and political issues. It applies to how we spend money, the way we use technology, our views on human rights, how we treat the environment, and so forth. While our focus must remain on liberation and full awakening, the world around us is the garden in which we grow merit and wisdom. The ethical conduct and compassion we cultivate cannot be intellectual; it must apply to our thoughts and actions here and now.

233

Being Truthful Doesn't Mean Being Rude

Your grandmother invites you for a homemade dinner, but she forgot that you don't like what she serves. When she asks, "How do you like the food?" do you say, "Grandma, I don't like it," which is the truth, or do you lie and reply, "It's really good," so she isn't offended?

Neither. The question she is really asking is, "I cooked this food because I love you. Are you receiving my love?" So when she asks about the food, you can reply, "Grandma, I appreciate so much your cooking dinner and I'm very happy to spend time with you. I really care about you." That is the truth, and it makes her much happier than saying you like her food, even if it's food you do like.

234

If We Care for Living Beings, We Must Also Care for the Environment

Living beings exist within environments. We are not independent of them; our bodies are made of the same elements found on the planet and nourished by food grown in the earth. If we care about ourselves, future generations, and all living beings, we must care about the environments in which we live. Thinking only about economic growth and inventing new technology because it's interesting, without thinking of how it will be used or the resources required to create it—the Earth cannot sustain such negligences.

Causing no harm is the meaning of ethical conduct; benefiting others is acting with compassion. Together these are the essence of the Dharma. We must live them, not simply mouth them.

235

The Importance of Aspirations

Making aspirations is a bodhisattva practice. Bodhisattvas aspire to do impossible things, and the force of their aspirations sets their minds in the right direction. Without aspirations, we won't set out to accomplish anything. Even if we can't fulfill our aspirations, we can at least make some progress toward them.

Each morning it's helpful to awaken with the aspiration not to harm others, to benefit them, and to generate bodhicitta.

Through habituation, some of our aspirations become determinations. Then our Dharma practice really takes off, because instead of just pondering, we take action. Beginning with an aspiration, we repeat it, transform it into a determination, and put it into action.

236

The Ache of Attachment

When fulfilled, attachment seems to bring great happiness; when unfulfilled, it causes great suffering. Unfortunately, we beings in cyclic existence cannot control all the causes and conditions that would fulfill all our wishes for worldly happiness and comfort. How then do we handle the ache of attachment?

One way is to imagine in your meditation that you get whatever you were craving. Envision your dream with all its details. Let yourself be taken away by imagining that you have the perfect situation. Then ask, *Will I be completely happy forever?*

The answer is invariably, "No." It's clear that satisfying our cravings with the perfect external situation doesn't lead to everlasting bliss. We must turn inward to find the true causes of happiness.

237

Give the Person to the Buddha

When plagued by the ache of attachment to a person, try this:

Imagine the Buddha in the space in front of you, and imagine the person you cling to next to the Buddha. From your heart, give that person to the Buddha—place that person in the Buddha's care. They are no longer yours, and the Buddha now looks after them.

If at first you feel sad, ask yourself, *Is that person better off under the Buddha's wise and compassionate guidance, or under my clinging attachment and expectations?*

The answer is clear. Again, from your heart, give the person to the Buddha and smile.

238

Speaking Out with Compassion

When politicians or other officials express opinions that we believe to be harmful or bigoted, we might react with anger. Nevertheless, if we wish to effect change, compassion is a more productive response than anger. For example, His Holiness the Dalai Lama advises Tibetans not to hate the Chinese Communists who have taken over Tibet and, in 1959, forced them into exile. He speaks out about the devastation that has occurred in Tibet since the takeover while being staunchly nonviolent in both his speech and actions.

Similarly, we must speak out against the views of people who are prejudiced against any group whatsoever. This can be done with strong and clear speech to counteract those views without hating or criticizing the people who have them. In other words, we separate the views from the people who have them. We speak about the distortion of those views and the harm that comes from holding them, without hating the people involved.

With compassion for everyone concerned, we can speak up: "This is not the way we want our country to be. Our country is inclusive."

239

Compassion Versus People-Pleasing

When we're trying to please people because we want their approval, there's no space in our mind for compassion. At that moment, our attention is on ourselves, anxiously worrying about whether we can do what we think they think we should do.

If we're always trying to second-guess people, to figure out what they want and to provide that, we're not being authentic with them because sometimes what they want harms them. To act compassionately, we must sometimes say "no" to their requests.

It's totally impossible to please other people in everything we do—they're never going to be completely happy with our actions. The whole process of trying to please people, win their approval, and get them to like us is basically self-centered.

240

Compassion as an Antidote to Low Self-Esteem

After learning the extent to which Westerners—even people who are considered successful by society—are subject to low self-esteem, His Holiness the Dalai Lama began to propose compassion for others as an antidote to self-denigration. At first this puzzled me: *Shouldn't I cultivate compassion toward myself first? How can I love others if I don't love myself?*

Upon thinking about it, however, I understood that when we focus on others' welfare, our mind is happier than when we ruminate on all the reasons why we don't measure up to what we think we should be. The self-talk about all our deficiencies is essentially conceptual rubbish and paying attention to the situation of others pulls us out of that. In addition, by reaching out to others with compassion, we feel good about ourselves.

When we can contribute to the well-being of others, our life has meaning.

241

The Kindness of Our Parents

If you had a difficult family life, one way to heal from it is to see that despite the chaos and neglect, kindness was also present. At the minimum, your parents gave us this body and if they were unable to take care of us themselves, they arranged for someone else to do so. The proof is that we are alive today. If they hadn't done this, we would have died in infancy.

Our parents did the best they could given the circumstances in which they grew up, the karmic seeds they brought into this life, and the fact that they are sentient beings under the influence of ignorance, anger, and attachment. They grew up in a certain historical time with forces beyond their control that shaped them. They may have had illness that they did not choose to have.

In short, let's accept our parents for who they are and the kindness they gave us. We are adults now and have the capacity to grow beyond whatever negative experiences we might have had as children. Let's appreciate our parents for doing the best they could and for giving us this body, the basis of precious human life, with its ability to progress on the path to awakening.

242

Two Ways of Seeing the Body

We view our bodies in different ways depending on the context and on the understanding we're trying to cultivate.

In the context of our precious human life in cyclic existence, the human body is special, to be taken care of because it's the basis upon which we can practice the Dharma and purify the mind.

In the context of our being enslaved by afflictions, karma, and the suffering we experience as a result, the body is seen as a source of duhkha. It is not something worth being attached to.

These two ways of seeing the body are not contradictory. We adopt one or the other depending on the understanding we want to cultivate in any given moment.

243

Our Precious Human Life

—

So many people ask me, "What should I do?" concerning problems in their relationships, work, status, and finances. They're often very confused, unable to see the situation clearly and make wise choices. This is because the mind clings to the happiness of this life, and we try to eke out all the temporal pleasure we can get out of it. Naturally, confusion sets in.

When we think deeply about the value and opportunity to transform our minds that our precious human life provides us, and then remember our mortality, our priorities become clear and we make good decisions. We use our limited time here on earth to do what is worthwhile instead of getting involved in things we may later regret.

244

Being Responsible for What Is Our Responsibility

~~~

Confused about what it means to be responsible, we often take responsibility for what isn't our responsibility, and don't take responsibility for what is our responsibility.

For example, when we make a general comment and another person takes it personally and gets upset, we think it's our fault, even though we meant no harm and the other person merely misunderstood what we said. Meanwhile, the other person blames us for hurting them. This is the opposite of how it should be. Others are responsible for their emotions, and we are responsible for our speech.

Similarly, if we are hurt, offended, or upset because of another person's words, we are responsible for our emotions and reactions. We cannot blame them for our anger. We have a choice of how to respond. Likewise, the other person is responsible for their speech and the intention behind it, no matter whether we are pleased or peeved by their words.

245

Aspiring for Buddhahood

—

We may be very inspired to benefit all sentient beings but know we're not capable of fulfilling that aspiration. We have some compassion and can make the commitment to get involved, but do we have the capability to carry things through? Do we have the knowledge and skills to actually benefit them?

We know that we're confused sentient beings ourselves. Although we can help now, our capacity and skill to help are limited. To carry out what we aspire to do, we must work on freeing ourselves from all hindrances and bad habits and develop all excellent qualities. Then the help we can give will be limitless.

This leads us to generate the precious bodhicitta, the aspiration to attain buddhahood for the benefit of all sentient beings.

246

A Simple Lifestyle

⁓

Whether we're laypeople or monastics, having the opportunity to live a simple lifestyle and having the discipline that will enable us to do so is a precious situation that will benefit society, future generations, and ourselves. Even a small group of individuals can impact the world by refraining from overconsumption and harming others, and from habituating the mind that's always saying *me, I, my,* and *mine,* to considering the feelings and needs of others.

Let's challenge our personal and collective suffering by consciously subduing and transforming our greedy, arrogant, and self-centered minds. This is done by deeply contemplating the fact that all others want happiness and want to avoid suffering as intensely as we do. Let's recall others' kindness to us as expressed in our interconnected world, and consider the disadvantages of self-centeredness and the benefits of cherishing others.

247

Being Misunderstood

Sometimes when we reach out to help others, they misinterpret our motivation and get upset with us. Other times people misunderstand our actions and lash out at us for no apparent reason. In such situations it's important to examine our motivation and see if we were negligent in any way or whether we had any subtle, unacknowledged hostility. If we discover we had a confused or hostile motivation, it's best to apologize.

However, if upon examination we find that our motivation was clear and we acted without any harmful intent, we must practice fortitude and realize that the other person is overcome by afflictions and buying into their karmic vision at that moment. We hold a compassionate attitude and try to communicate as best as we can. Sometimes it's best to give that person some space, because it's difficult to connect when their mind is in that state.

248

Buddha-Nature

We must differentiate between a person's harmful actions and the person who did them. The action might be abhorrent, but that doesn't mean the person who did it is evil. Why? Because that person has buddha-nature, the possibility to become fully awakened. The fundamental nature of their mind is pure and untainted and can never be defiled. Saying a person is evil or hopeless is like saying the Buddha lied when he taught that all sentient beings have the possibility to become fully awakened.

Knowing that we all have the pure nature of mind, we respect others and ourselves. We can still say that what somebody did was harmful, but we don't have to hate them for doing it, just like we can still say, "I made a mistake," but it doesn't mean we are awful people.

249

Glass Half-Full

~

A friend told me they found a frog on the golf course. One of its legs was stuck in a sprinkler, and it was doomed to die if it stayed there. They cut off the frog's leg to keep it alive, brought it home, and nurtured it. They had a little pond where the frog lived for four months until there was a sudden freeze and the frog froze to death.

When I heard this, my heart went, *Oh no! The poor frog died just like that.*

My friend said, "How wonderful that it came and lived with us for four months."

What an example of seeing the glass half-full instead of half-empty! My friend talked about all the living beings on their land with love, joy, and total acceptance of their impermanence. What a wonderful Dharma perspective!

250

Acknowledging Our Mistakes

⁓

If someone were to come along and tell us we had a nose on our face, would we get angry? No. Why not? Because our nose is obvious. It's there for all the world to see. Someone merely saw and commented on it.

Our faults and mistakes are similar. They're obvious, and people see them. A person noticing them is merely commenting on what is evident to everyone. Why should we get angry? We'd be more relaxed if we acknowledged our errors and faults. "You're right. I made a mistake." Or, "Yes, I have that bad habit." Instead of putting on a show of "I'm perfect, how dare you say that!" we could just admit our errors and apologize.

Having faults means we're normal, not hopeless. Oftentimes, acknowledging our errors and apologizing defuses a situation.

251

Parents and Kids

~

Parents want the best for their children and that may take the form of giving kids everything they want. But that puts the children at a disadvantage in life, because they won't always get what they want and they'll have no practice in dealing with the frustration of life not happening the way they would like it to.

Far better is for parents to show through their own example how to deal with frustration without blaming or holding grudges. If parents take it a step further and take others' feelings, needs, and concerns into consideration, they will do their children a great favor by modeling kind and considerate behavior for them.

252

Happier with Less

~

Psychological studies have found that we judge our happiness and wealth in comparison to that of those around us. If we all go down a notch together, everyone will feel that they have enough and nobody will get jealous.

By preserving the earth's resources and not consuming as much, we'll be more creative about entertainment; we'll do more activities with our family and friends and share more intimately with each other. The stronger relationships we will build in this process will bring much more happiness than filling our rooms with stuff we don't need and then getting upset because we can't get the next new thing we don't need.

Instead of worrying about the economy, let's cultivate satisfaction with what we have. That brings peace to the mind.

253

Compassion Versus Foolishness

Compassion doesn't mean we allow someone to abuse us. In cases of domestic violence, saying, "You beat me yesterday, but I forgive you, so you can beat me tomorrow, too," is not compassion, it's foolishness. If someone is harming us or our children, we should make it very clear to the person that this behavior is not acceptable, and we should immediately leave the situation. It helps neither us nor the other person if we allow the situation to continue. We must protect ourselves and prevent the other person from creating destructive karma that will ripen in their suffering later.

Compassion entails being strong. Without being angry at the other person, we must be clear about what is appropriate behavior and what is not, and convey this to everyone else involved.

254

Equanimity

Equanimity involves freeing our mind from bias and prejudice. We shed our attachments to dear ones, our animosity toward enemies, and our apathy for strangers, and instead train our mind to see everyone as equal in terms of wanting happiness and not suffering. Looking beyond superficial appearances, we see into others' hearts, where our commonality as sentient beings lies. In terms of our feelings, we train to see everyone as worthwhile and cultivate a sense of openhearted concern for them equally.

But that doesn't mean we treat everyone the same way. We still pay attention to social relationships and others' capabilities and knowledge.

255

Trust

It's important to give each individual the trust that is appropriate for them. We don't trust a two-year-old with matches, but we do trust an adult. We don't trust an untrained person to fly a plane, but we do trust a trained pilot. If someone has a lot of emotional swings, we don't expect them to always be available to help us when we need someone to talk to. Knowing someone has a substance-abuse problem, we don't give them money when they make a desperate plea for our immediate generosity.

Each person is trustworthy in different areas of life. Our job is to find out what those areas are and to give them the appropriate level of trust in those areas. It is not kindness to give someone more trust than they can bear; that could lead to disappointment on our side and feelings of failure for the other person.

256

Disappointment

⁓

Although we try to accurately assess people's trustworthiness in different areas of life, sometimes we err and expect too much from them. When they don't act the way we trusted or expected them to act, we feel angry and disappointed, sometimes even betrayed.

There's a saying I remember in these situations to calm my mind and return to a more realistic outlook: "Sentient beings do what sentient beings do." That is, beings in cyclic existence who are under the control of ignorance, attachment, and animosity don't always act in predictable ways; they sometimes lack good judgment or act in ways that sabotage their own well-being. Rather than be shocked by such behavior, I should understand that it happens. If I didn't cling to the unrealistic expectation that this person should be perfect, I wouldn't be so upset when they aren't. I need to accept what is.

257

Just Do Your Practice

~

Stop waiting for grandiose flashes of insight to occur, or for instances of deep samadhi. Don't wait to have a vision of the Buddha that you can tell everyone about. Just be content with doing your practice.

258

What Should I Do?

⁓

When we're angry or upset, we want to know, *What should I do? I need to do something!* But when the mind is turbulent and confused, we can't see the situation clearly. That's not the time to decide what to do. That's the time to calm our mind.

When the mind is calm, it's possible to look at the situation and see how to respond in a constructive way. When the mind is calm, it often doesn't take long to formulate a plan of action.

259

Birds of a Feather

As we practice the Dharma, it's natural that our friendships will change. Some of our old friendships may continue, but we may also find a new circle of friends.

In any case, the old saying "Birds of a feather flock together" is true. As our mind turns away from usual sources of entertainment and distraction, we'll seek out people who share our interests. We'll want to be around people who encourage our virtuous qualities and actions, who comment when we're being negligent, and who help us work with our anger and jealousy. We'll want to have friends who live with good, ethical conduct and who encourage us to do the same.

Good friends who understand and support our spiritual yearnings are rare; we should treasure them.

260

Practicing without Pushing

Our school systems are often driven by reward and punishment based on individual effort. We sometimes bring this same mentality into the Dharma and think, *I've got to practice to please my teacher or to meet somebody's expectations.* That's the mind looking for reward.

Alternatively, we may think, *I've got to practice, otherwise I'm a failure. I'll have a horrible rebirth.* That's the mind afraid of punishment.

Both of these motivations—to seek reward and avoid punishment—are not conducive to practicing the Dharma with a happy mind. They only lead to pushing ourselves and getting frazzled as a result.

Joyous effort is based on understanding the spiritual path. It's an attitude that sees the benefit our practice will bring for ourselves and others and, without pushing, takes delight in doing what's constructive.

261

How to Practice Joyous Effort

The Buddha spoke of four ways of practicing joyous effort:

First, when harmful mental states arise, apply the antidotes and subdue them.

Second, prevent harmful mental states from arising by habituating ourselves with beneficial perspectives.

Third, enrich beneficial emotions and views that have arisen by rejoicing in our virtue and continuing to familiarize ourselves with those actions and mental states.

Fourth, generate beneficial emotions and views that have yet to arise by encouraging ourselves and continuing to study, reflect, and meditate.

262

Celebrating Birthdays

On our birthdays, we command all the attention, but the day should actually be about expressing gratitude to our parents or whoever raised us. They gave us this body, kept us alive as infants, and raised us. They made sure we got an education and taught us manners. Our birthday means we're a year closer to death, so why are we celebrating?

Having a precious human life with all the conditions necessary to progress on the path to awakening *is* worthy of celebration. We should thank all the people we were in previous lives for creating the virtuous causes for our present life; we should thank our parents for giving us this body, our teachers for educating us, and our spiritual mentors for guiding our Dharma studies and practice.

Birthdays are joyous not because we receive presents, but because we celebrate all the kindness others have shown us.

263

What the Body Is

When we understand the body—its causes, nature, and results—we stop relating to it in terms of attachment or aversion. We let go of thinking this body is beautiful and will bring us ultimate pleasure. We also let go of thinking this body is evil and sinful and must be punished. Both of these views are to be abandoned because they're unrealistic ways of seeing the body.

Mindfulness of the body reveals that it exists by being merely designated in dependence on a collection of selfless parts. There is no inherently existent body to hate or to be attached to.

With this understanding, we will make wise decisions about what is valuable in our lives and how to relate to our bodies in a realistic and beneficial way.

264

Reacting to Your Feelings

Observe that if you react to an unpleasant feeling with hostility, your mind becomes angry, which brings more unpleasant feelings.

Observe that if you experience a pleasant feeling, attachment arises. You want more, and soon your mind is spinning with plans to get what you desire so you can experience more pleasurable feelings. With attachment and aversion toward pleasant and unpleasant feelings respectively, you are like a bull with a rope tied to a ring in its nose; you have no freedom.

Now try to observe the pleasurable or painful feelings without reacting, without making a story about the feelings or the object. When you can do this, your mind becomes calmer.

265

Observing the Mind

A key part of Dharma practice is observing what is going on in our mind at any given time: what thoughts and emotions are arising? As you observe the thoughts and emotions that arise, ask yourself, *Where do they come from? Where were they before they arose in my mind?* While they manifest, investigate, *Where do they exist while they are present?* And finally, after they cease, *Where did they go?*

This helps us to be less reactive and attached to chaotic thoughts and emotions.

266

Bodhicitta Begins with Toilet Paper

We all want to learn how to open our hearts to benefit other living beings and know that our actions matter and influence other people. This is where toilet paper comes in. When we finish the toilet-paper roll, do we install a new roll, or do we just leave a bare cardboard cylinder and let the next person who comes in replace it? If the latter, it leaves others in a compromised position.

Great compassion starts with simple things like toilet paper.

267

The Day We Take Refuge

The day we take refuge in the Three Jewels in a ceremony is a very special day in our lives.

Taking refuge entails being clear about our spiritual path and our purpose and direction in life. By taking precepts, we make a major decision about what actions we want and don't want to do in life. We arrive at these decisions voluntarily due to our own wisdom, by contemplating what has worked in our life so far and what hasn't.

Feeling comfortable about taking refuge and precepts indicates spiritual and personal growth. We are setting ourselves in a worthwhile and positive direction and are progressing step-by-step.

268

Rejoicing in the Precepts

We often don't realize that having the opportunity to take precepts, whether for one day or for life, is very rare and requires a lot of merit.

Just think how many people will spend their time today talking about unimportant things, speaking harsh words, or coveting each other's belongings without a second thought.

When you take precepts, rejoice in your virtue and commitment to create peace in the lives of the people around you and in the world. At the end of each day, dedicate the merit of taking and keeping the precepts, sending it in all directions. Think of it as white light radiating from your heart, touching every living being and bringing peace to their lives. Dedicate your practice of ethical conduct for the long-term benefit and awakening of each and every sentient being.

269

Creating the Causes for Wealth

After a discussion on generosity, I gave people the assignment to go through their closet and give away the things they didn't use. This was more difficult than it looked. Some people couldn't even get into their closets. Some got in there and discovered things they'd forgotten about, but after seeing those things they became attached to them all over again. Some got a few items into a box but couldn't get the box into their car. Some put the boxes in their trunk but couldn't go to a charity to offer them. Always there was some obstacle.

Clearly, the self-centered, miserly mind was at play in these situations. Unfortunately, this attitude creates the karmic cause for us to be poor. We don't need to empty out our house, but let's not pass up the opportunity to create the karmic cause for wealth by practicing generosity. Let's remember how good it feels to see someone's face light up when they receive our gifts.

270

Please Tell Me the Truth

When someone lies to me, I feel offended because it seems to me that they don't trust me to know the truth. Perhaps they fear I will be disappointed in them or judge them.

Please tell me the truth. I can handle it. What I don't like is the breakdown in trust between us when you lie to me.

271

Seeing a Pure Land

Our environment is a reflection of our mind. We're born into a certain environment due to the karma we've created in previous lives. How we relate to our present environment also comes from our mind. How we think and feel is up to us.

For example, when the snow falls, we can see the snowflakes as many Chenrezigs—the Buddha of Compassion —falling and dissolving into us, bringing bliss and compassion into our mind. Or we can be disgruntled and think, *Ugh, I hate snow.* In fact, snow doesn't exist as beautiful or awful from its own side. The more we can imagine our environment as a pure land and make it one by caring for the environment and the beings in it, the more we create the karmic cause to be reborn in a pure land.

Our environment, our mind, our karma—all these are interrelated.

272

Going Out for a Meal

Going out for a meal can be a time to connect with others —and with a pot of attachment and confusion.

First you discuss for twenty minutes what type of food you want: Italian, Chinese, or Mexican? Another fifteen minutes to choose which restaurant to go to. Upon arriving at the restaurant, you spend twenty minutes discussing with your friends what to order. Calling the waiter or waitress over, you ask, "Can you make this dish without this ingredient, and add this ingredient to this other dish?" Once the food comes, you talk with your friends and eat without paying much attention to the food. After the meal, you say, "I ate so much, I feel sick. But it was so delicious."

It's more rewarding to eat a simple meal, connect with friends, and express gratitude to all those who cooked and served the meal.

273

Death, the Great Equalizer

There's no place to go where we're immune to death. Yet now that we can send a spacecraft to Pluto to take photographs, for sure somebody's thinking, *Maybe if we send people to Pluto they won't die* . . .

That won't work because just having a body under the control of afflictions and karma means it is in the process of decaying and will eventually cease, regardless of where it is in the universe.

Death is definite. Throughout history people have died, and there's no reason that we're going to be an exception. Even holy beings die. It happens to everybody. Our social class, education, privilege or no privilege—all these don't matter. Death is the great equalizer. It happens to everyone.

This knowledge need not be depressing. When seen correctly, it is enlivening. We see that greed and hatred have no benefit in the long term. We set good priorities and live by them. We live in a meaningful way and care for others.

274

Preparing for Death—the Practicalities

Some people believe that being spiritual means ignoring worldly concerns to the point of being impractical. Actually, as spiritual practitioners we must take care of important practical aspects of life, otherwise we risk bringing distress to others when we die.

For example, since we will die eventually, it makes sense to have a will, so that while we're actively dying we don't have to think about what will happen to our possessions. Designating a power of attorney to take care of financial matters should we become incapacitated is also wise. To prevent relatives from having to make medical decisions for us that they are loathe to make, it is wise to make a living will or advance directive detailing our medical wishes should we be unable to express them ourselves.

275

Preparing for Death Emotionally

—

Making peace in our minds with those whom we have harmed or been harmed by opens our hearts, whereas dying with unresolved regrets or unexpressed love brings anguish. Since the time of our death is uncertain and unknown, it behooves us to tell our dear ones how much we appreciate and care for them and to make amends and resolve bad feelings with those we have hurt.

276

Apologizing and Forgiving

⁓

Apologizing and forgiving also helps us complete unfinished business before we die. Apologizing is expressing sorrow that we didn't meet our own standards for good conduct and, as a result, harmed others. Forgiving is letting go of the anger and resentment we may hold toward those who have harmed us. None of us want to die with anger and resentment; apologizing to those we need to apologize to and forgiving those we need to forgive enables us to die without regret. Both apologizing and forgiving require courage—not physical bravery as in war, but deep, inner courage that brings inner and outer harmony. Such harmony brings peace to ourselves and others.

277

Preparing for Death Spiritually

Depending on how we have practiced during our lives, we will rely on different methods of practice at the time of death.

Taking refuge in the Three Jewels and generating bodhicitta will assuredly bring good results at the time of death. Thinking of the excellent qualities of the Three Jewels and entrusting ourselves to their guidance, our mind will be free of manifest afflictions. Visualizing the Buddha and/or bodhisattvas, we will remember their qualities. This activates the seeds of those qualities in our own mind, and this protects us from the ripening of destructive karma.

Generating bodhicitta frees the mind from the bonds of the self-centeredness that could bring anxiety and angst while dying. The aspiration to benefit all sentient beings in the highest way, bodhicitta is an aspiration that directs our consciousness to a good rebirth in future lives, where we can continue the path to full awakening.

278

Like a Bird Taking Off

From a Dharma viewpoint, the body is simply the basis for having a precious human life. That's all. We don't need to pamper it. We don't need to do ascetic trips. Just keep it clean and take care of it so we can use it to practice the Dharma. Then when it's time to die, we leave.

Lama Yeshe used to say that when we die we want to be like a bird taking off from a ship in the middle of the ocean. The bird just flies. It doesn't think, *Oh dear, can I fly off this ship?* It doesn't start flapping its wings and looking back, thinking, *Oh, this precious ship . . . How can I leave you?* It just goes—smoothly, gracefully, with no regrets.

279

Dharma and Religious Institutions

~

Religious institutions are formed by human beings, so they're bound to undergo difficulties. Our job is to deepen our refuge and transform our hearts and minds. Religious institutions are for the purpose of uniting practitioners, encouraging us to practice, and helping us to keep true to the teachings. Aside from that, religious institutions are not valuable. In other words, our purpose is not to create and reinforce a religious institution for its own sake. Our practice does not entail becoming a cheerleader for our own religion: "My religion is the best! Come join it!" Our aim is inner transformation; we want to become buddhas, not officials of an institution. Don't confuse genuine spiritual practice with religious institutions.

If our refuge is in a religious institution, when the institution or its officials have problems, our refuge gets shaky. But when our refuge is in the Buddha, the Dharma, and the Sangha, our faith will not be affected by controversies created by ordinary human beings. We can bring compassion and wisdom to those problems without getting discouraged.

280

Speaking the Truth

Trust is a key element in having good relationships, and speaking truthfully is an important element in creating trust. The ancient Buddhist philosopher Nagarjuna says that speech is only the truth when spoken with a good motivation, so telling someone all the things we don't like about them is not truthful speech. It would be more appropriate to speak about the difficulties we have in relating to that person, without blaming them for our own bad feelings.

Another element of truthful speech is to abandon actions that we are ashamed of. If we do that, there won't be things we want to cover up by lying. If we have done things that we regret, frankly and humbly admitting them, apologizing, and making amends are signs of integrity and courage and help to restore trust.

281

The Big Picture

The self-centered mind makes everything that happens to "me" get blown out of proportion. A scholar in Dharamsala spoke about the illness he had suffered from for one year. When he was lying in bed, unable to do much, he asked himself, *What is the big picture? There's what's in front of me, what's behind me, and what's on both sides. What's in front is future lives. What's behind is previous lives. On both sides are other sentient beings' experiences.*

When he started thinking like this, his mind relaxed because he saw that whatever suffering he was experiencing was actually quite small compared to the big picture of all sentient beings, and the big picture of his own past and future lives.

282

Two Ears, One Mouth

It's said that the fact that we have two ears and one mouth indicates what we need to do more of. Listening from the heart is a skill we need to develop. It is motivated by compassion and demonstrated by making eye contact, leaning toward the speaker, and not interrupting. Listening is not a passive activity. The way we listen can either encourage or discourage the speaker from sharing. If we interrupt someone to give our two cents, if we discredit what they say and tell them they shouldn't feel what they feel, we may say a lot of words but actual communication will be absent.

Very often people just need to be heard. When we listen because we sincerely care, that comes through to the speaker by our body language. Even if a conversation starts out with tension, if we listen with careful attention, that tension will ease because the other person feels understood.

283

The Importance of Humor

Humor is crucial to practice the Dharma. Sometimes we take ourselves so seriously, digging ourselves into a self-absorbed, self-critical ditch of discouragement that is really unnecessary. Learning to laugh at ourselves is a gift because sometimes the way our mind thinks is really hilarious.

One day I was meditating while in retreat and the thought popped into my mind, *My teacher probably has clairvoyant powers and knows how well I'm meditating and how nicely my practice is progressing.*

I immediately started to laugh. My thought was perfect proof of how poorly I was meditating! As they say, back to the drawing board . . .

284

Virtuous Restraint

Restraining ourselves from nonvirtuous actions is itself a virtuous action. When we take precepts, we make a firm determination not to do certain actions. Every moment we're not doing those actions, we're accumulating the merit of abandoning nonvirtuous actions.

Two people may be sitting in a room, one with the precept to abandon stealing and the other without this precept. Both people are not stealing at that moment, but the person with the precept accumulates merit by just sitting there because they are actively not stealing. The other person does not accumulate merit because they have not made the conscious decision to abandon stealing.

The longer you keep precepts, the more you will feel the base of virtue supporting you.

285

A True Revolution

If we really value freedom, we must create a free state in our heart by opposing ignorance, anger, and attachment. Ignorance is the dictator that won't let any freedom exist in our mind; greed and animosity are its henchmen. We need to bring the same spirit and fervor for overthrowing ignorance's oppressive regime that some Americans feel on the Fourth of July and that people in India feel on Republic Day, the date on which the Constitution of India came into effect. In this case, however, the oppressive regime we're going to overthrow is our self-grasping ignorance. Instead of throwing tea into the Boston Harbor, we must throw our attachment and hatred overboard. Then we can bask in genuine freedom.

Let's approach Dharma practice with the same enthusiasm.

286

Subtle Impermanence

There are two types of impermanence: gross and subtle. We can see gross impermanence with our senses—the sun rises, people die, a bridge collapses. Although these events appear to happen suddenly, they depend on subtle, gradual change. The earth slowly moves around the sun; the person and the bridge have been aging for a long time.

Subtle impermanence means that things arise, abide, and cease in every nanosecond. They never remain the same in the next moment. When we observe, we can't find a split nanosecond. We may have the image of one discreet moment, a second discreet moment, and so on, as if there were nice little discreet moments with invisible glue holding them together to form a solid continuity. However, it's not like that. We can't actually find when one moment ends and a new one begins—it's just our conceptual mind that divides the flow of time into units.

When we think deeply about things changing from moment to moment, the question arises, "What goes from one moment to the next? If a grain of sand, for example, isn't the same in the next moment, what makes both of them grains of sand? Is there an essence that goes from one moment to the next?"

This leads us to investigate phenomena's deeper mode of existence: their emptiness of inherent existence. This is the key to eliminating ignorance and the doorway to awakening.

287

Discovering Who We Aren't

Humankind's perpetual question is: *Who am I?* As individuals we create all sorts of identities based on race, ethnicity, sex, gender, sexual orientation, socioeconomic class, educational level, religion, nationality, and so on. We believe that we are all these identities, and that brings a certain sense of security, false as it may be.

In Buddhist practice we endeavor to discover not who we are, but who we are not. We are not all those fabricated identities. When we go in search of our essence, we don't find any of those identities. In fact, we don't find anything that we can draw a line around and say, "This is forever and ever *me*."

Although this understanding may be initially unnerving, it leads us to freedom.

288

Freedom in Not Finding

⁓

The song "She Carries Me" by Jennifer Berezan is an ode to the bodhisattva Kuan Yin (Avalokiteshvara, the Buddha of Compassion). One line says, "I have no name. I have no home," poignantly reminding us of times in our life when we felt bereft of love, belonging, or connection.

But I've found solace in having no name and no home when name and home refer to an inherently existent *I* or *me* that is found amid an inherently existent group of people who share an identity and want to protect and preserve that identity. Those concrete notions of "I am this" bind us. Other forms of identity demand our allegiance to ideas or values that we may not agree with. Still others expect us to act in particular ways that restrict us from living according to our own values and principles.

Being without a name or home frees us from our own distorted conceptions as well as from others' narrow expectations.

289

Is There an I Sitting Here?

We feel that there's an inherently existent *me* sitting here: "I am *me*." We don't feel that we exist only because the causes for us existed. Rather, we feel as if we're an independent entity, unrelated to causes and conditions and any other factors.

Similarly, we believe there is a "solid" person here. Yes, there is the body and mind. But in addition, somewhere mixed in the body and mind, there is a *me*.

But as soon as we begin to examine whether the *I* exists independently, we see that it's impossible for the *I* to exist in that way. If the *I* were independent of all other factors, we could not change. But we do change. That means we're dependent on causes and conditions. Being dependent, we can't exist independently or inherently.

290

We Just Don't See It

My teacher Lama Yeshe used to say to us, "Emptiness, the ultimate truth, is not somewhere far away in another universe. It's right here, dear. You are not separate from it."

It's our very nature, we just don't see it.

291

To See and Not to See

A line in a Buddhist scripture reads, "Not seeing is the best seeing." Huh? What does *that* mean?

Unlike seeing emptiness—the absence of inherent existence—this line means not seeing or finding inherent existence when we search for the ultimate mode of existence. The wisdom that realizes such a false way of existing does not exist at all is the best seeing. By not seeing inherent existence, that wisdom sees emptiness; it directly and nondeceptively sees reality.

292

Slippery Speech

⁓

We should take care to present issues in ways that others can understand, but we must also ensure that we don't misrepresent situations.

For example, we might have forgotten to do something, but when somebody asks us, we say, "I was going to check later to see if it was still necessary," instead of simply admitting we forgot.

When people ask us about our behavior, we may explain it in a way that presents ourselves positively, thinking, *This is so they'll understand. I don't want to make this into a big deal.* But if we look more closely at our motivation, we might find that we're actually trying to avoid blame by actively diverting someone's attention or covering up our actions.

It's good to pay attention to these subtle aspects of truthful speech.

293

Just Be Kind

A friend told me her story of going to the doctor after not feeling well for some weeks. The doctor ran some tests and then called her in and gave her a devastating diagnosis: she had a terminal illness, and she was only in her early thirties.

Her initial reaction was panic, grief, and fear. Then she asked herself, *What would His Holiness the Dalai Lama do if this happened to him?* And three simple words came to her: *Just be kind.* She took that advice and practiced being kind to her worried family and to the doctors, nurses, and other medical staff who cared for her. She practiced kindness to the other patients in the hospital and to their relatives and friends, as well.

Her mind was peaceful and satisfied. She came to accept her upcoming death.

Meanwhile, the doctor ran some more tests and came back with the results: there was a misdiagnosis. Her illness was treatable, not terminal.

294

Fear of the Future

Fear of the future when we're sick, injured, or dying throws the mind into pandemonium. But the future hasn't happened yet. We're terrified of what presently does not exist.

If we're lying in a hospital bed, we can reflect, *There are kind people around me who are helping me.* If we're in pain, we can think, *I'm in pain, but there are people around who understand my situation and are trying to alleviate the pain. Plus, I have the power of my Dharma practice to help pacify my mind.* With compassion, we aspire, *May my pain suffice for the pain of all other living beings.* We can practice the taking-and-giving meditation, imagining taking on others' suffering, using it to destroy our own ignorance and self-centered attitude, and then, with love, imagining giving our body, possessions, and merit to others, bringing them peace and joy.

It's not easy, but with practice we can train the mind to focus on what is important instead of flying off into self-centered, conceptual, whirling mental fabrications. Then difficult situations will be manageable.

295

Meditating Alone

Many of us have had the urge to go to the mountains and meditate alone, thinking, *If only I could meditate far away from all these obnoxious sentient beings, I could quiet my mind, gain realizations, and be peaceful. Then I could really benefit others.*

Wherever we are, whatever we're doing, as long as our mind is in cyclic existence, there are going to be difficulties. But if we have a gracious attitude, one of acceptance, kindness, and compassion, then even the sentient beings that we don't get along with cease to cause us problems.

We see this in His Holiness the Dalai Lama and in the lives of the great masters. Their inspiring biographies point us back to our own practice and to transforming the mind wherever we are.

296

Kindness and Interdependence

⁓

Our interdependence is a source of kindness.

To understand this, take something you use—your phone, for example—and trace back how many living beings were involved in its creation. People designed the phone, and its parts were manufactured by workers in many countries. Each part was made of special materials. Some of those materials were mined from the earth by people who spent the better part of each day in mine shafts or open pits. Other elements were made by people who created these new materials. People transported the various parts from one place to another, and still more people were involved in designing the trucks, ships, railroads, or planes that moved them. Still more people packaged the phone and built the store where you bought it.

Thinking of everyone who has been involved for us to have a phone, we get a sense of the kindness of all those living beings. Whether they had the intention to benefit us in particular doesn't matter. What's important is that due to their efforts, we have the things we need to stay alive and to prosper.

That, in and of itself, indicates that we are each the recipients of great kindness.

297

The Unreal World

When we look at the world and the people around us, and even at ourselves, everything seems so real. There are real people, real problems, real happiness, and real blame. But all of this—ourselves included—exist by being merely designated in dependence on a collection of parts and attributes. Our mind contributes to creating all these things; it conceives the various pieces as one object that performs a certain function and gives it a name.

For example, someone becomes an employee of a business establishment because of passing a job interview and being hired. She was not born an employee; she becomes one because as a society we have agreed that if a company decides to hire someone, that person becomes an employee. We have also agreed that "employee" has a certain definition that fits this person. But there is no employee inside this person's body or mind, and we can't find an employee separate from her body and mind. An employee appears when we don't analyze, but we can't find it when we do analyze how it really exists.

Things exist nominally; they aren't objective, fixed entities "out there." When this understanding is applied to us, our body and mind, and all other phenomena, our perspective softens and broadens. We relax.

298

My and Mine

⌒

When a car is at the car dealer's, we may admire it, but if it gets dented or scratched it doesn't bother us because it belongs to the dealership. But after we buy the car and take it home, we call it "mine." Then, if it is damaged we are incensed: "Someone damaged *my* car!"

It's the same car as before, but now, because we consider it "mine," it takes on a whole new meaning. But what about the car is mine? Is there something inside one of the parts or inside the car as a whole that makes it mine?

"Mine" is only a designation we give to something that as a society we agree is legally possessed by a particular person. In fact, there is nothing findable in that object itself that makes it mine.

299

My Child

When the neighbor's child flunks the spelling test in first grade, it's not a problem for us, but if our own child does, it's a big deal. "Oh no, he won't get into a good university or have a good career!"

We feel special affection for our own children. What makes those people "mine"? If it were genes, then when we looked at genes under a microscope we would instantly recognize them as "mine." Is it because we have some physical resemblance? If so, then other people whom we don't know but who have similar physical characteristics to us would appear to be "mine."

When we examine closely, we can't find any objective criteria that makes another person "mine." In fact, if the babies were mixed up in the hospital, we would feel that the child who wasn't our biological progeny is "mine." "Mine" is only a designation given by our mind.

We don't need to obsessively worry about our children and be helicopter parents because they are "mine." They'll be fine. After all, they can use spell-check.

300

Watching Our Words

~

When people say, "I'm overwhelmed," we think we know what this means, but do we ever analyze how it feels to be overwhelmed or where that feeling comes from?

When I say, "I'm overwhelmed," my whole paradigm shifts to, "It's too much, don't ask anything more from me, I can't do it. Leave me alone." I don't have the energy to do what I feel overwhelmed by, but I sure can dig in my heels and have a pity party.

Another common expression is, "I need my own space." Do we mean physical space or mental space? Can somebody give us mental space? All of us want or need "my space," but what exactly is it?

Reflecting in this way illustrates how the words we choose shape our experience of a situation. In the same situation one person may feel overwhelmed, another needs space, and a third person exhibits joyous effort.

What words would accompany joyous effort?

301

Going on a Picnic

~

For great practitioners, death is like going on a picnic. My preceptor, Kyabje Ling Rinpoche, spent thirteen days in clear light meditation after his breath stopped. The clear light mind—the subtlest level of consciousness—remained in his body during that time while he meditated on the emptiness of inherent existence, the ultimate nature of reality. When his meditation was complete, the consciousness left the body, which then slumped over.

This is the kind of person we aspire to be when we die—not one who craves and clings to this life and its body, possessions, and loved ones. Wouldn't it be wonderful at death to think, *How nice! Meditation in the clear light. Now I can go forward and continue working for the benefit of sentient beings in future lives!*

To be able to relax and enjoy death, we need to release our craving and attachment day by day. Whenever they arise, we must reflect, *This is not something worth clinging to. There is a higher purpose in my life.*

302

The Benefit of Compassion Goes to the Giver

———

His Holiness the Dalai Lama explains that the actual benefit and joy of compassion goes more to the compassionate person than to the recipient of that compassion: If our hearts have compassion, we are delighted to have the opportunity to benefit others, to connect with them, and to relate with kindness. We feel good about ourselves as well as about the other person.

On the other hand, the recipient of compassion may or may not feel happy. If their mind is sunk in self-concern, they may not be able to see our compassion for what it is. In short, their benefiting from my compassion is not certain, but my benefiting from it is assured.

303

The Kindness of Others

~

Contemplating the kindness of our parents and then recalling that all sentient beings have been our parents in previous lives is one way to cultivate a sense of closeness with others. Some people have had unhappy family lives, and so this meditation may be difficult for them. In that case, it is recommended to think of the kindness of whoever took care of us when we were young.

When we were infants we couldn't take care of ourselves at all; we couldn't feed ourselves, cover ourselves with a blanket if we were cold, get water when we were thirsty, or change our diapers. Others did that for us. They even woke up in the middle of the night to feed us when we wailed. As we got older, they taught us to speak and taught us how to be polite and behave properly with others. They made sure we got an education and encouraged whatever talents or interests we had.

It's important for our own emotional health and spiritual progress to let the knowledge of this kindness into our hearts.

304

Why Did You Do That?

~

When we're upset with someone, we often ask them, "Why did you do that?"

Before we ask that question, let's first ask ourselves whether it really is important why they did that action. Are we, instead, asking that question rhetorically? As a way of accusing someone so we can be angry no matter what they say?

Sometimes we may need to understand why somebody did something in order to work out a better way of doing it. But it's usually more pertinent and effective to talk about ourselves and what we feel without imputing motivations and meanings onto others' words and actions.

305

The Perfection of Generosity

Generosity is a virtue that everyone respects. It's a fundamental way in which people connect with each other in all countries and cultures, and it exemplifies how dependent we are on one another. Giving bonds us together; through it, we share resources that enrich others' lives. Being generous makes us feel good about ourselves and frees us from the strangulation of miserliness.

An important factor in giving is to give without expectation of return, of receiving even a thank you. That can be challenging at times, especially when we crave appreciation or at least recognition. But craving a "reward" takes the joy out of giving and can even lead us to regret our generosity, which destroys the merit we created.

The trick is to let the generous action itself be the reward. The feeling of an open heart is in itself the greatest benefit we can receive from giving, so focus on that and leave all other expectations behind.

306

Pure Generosity

~

The extent to which we cultivate four factors when practicing generosity mirrors the joy and merit we create. These four are: giving with a pure motivation, giving with respect, giving with skill, and giving to dedicate the merit of our generosity.

The first factor is to have a pure motivation, one free of any intention to hurt or manipulate the recipient. Such a motivation demonstrates respect for the recipient; it is not condescending or arrogant at all. It is also free from expectation, such as wanting a good reputation on account of being rich or praise for being generous.

I was with my teacher at his monastery in South India when a beggar came to his room. Geshela got up—he was overweight, so standing up from sitting on the floor was not so easy— went in another room, and came back with a new blanket, which he respectfully handed to the beggar. The beggar—an old, thin man—grinned and hobbled away. Geshela returned to his room as if nothing had happened, as if giving new blankets to beggars was something he did every day.

307

Giving with Respect

—

The second factor in making generosity wonderful is to give in a respectful manner—not to complain when people ask for help or make a show of being kind. It also involves how we give—giving in a respectful manner, not simply tossing an article at the recipient.

A friend told me of his experience in Berkeley, California, where many street people sit on the sidewalk asking for money. A woman with her head down caught his attention, and he pulled out a dollar. With both hands, he gave it to her while saying, "I wish I could give you more, but this is what I have now."

She lifted her head and there were tears in her eyes. He realized that she valued being respected as a human being more than she valued the money.

308

Giving with Skill and Dedication

Great skill is also needed when giving—we should give only what will benefit that person and will not harm another living being. Do not give weapons or poisons; do not kill an animal to feed either a person or another animal; do not give intoxicants.

The fourth factor in giving is to dedicate the merit of your generosity. Just as you had a pure motivation to benefit the other person and to progress on the path to full awakening for the benefit of all beings, dedicate for that same purpose.

309

Giving Material Possessions and Money

The giving of money and possessions is the most common type of generosity. When giving material goods, whenever possible give things of good quality that the other person needs. Don't give money if you think that the person will use it to purchase drugs, alcohol, or weapons, or to gamble. If someone has a substance-abuse problem, offer to take them to a treatment center instead.

If you aren't sure how a person will use the money, give food. It's good to carry protein bars or fruit to share with people living on the streets. In some countries the beggars that surround tourists are often so numerous that if you give to one, you will be swamped. So give when it is suitable and safe.

It will not be possible to support all the charities whose work you admire, so select a few that use the money wisely. When you don't have much to give, remember that it is your motivation, not the amount, that makes the action one of generosity.

310

Giving Protection

Giving protection helps those who are lost or in danger. For example, help travelers by giving them proper directions and helping them arrive safely at their destination. Rescue insects that are about to drown in water. If you suspect someone is being trafficked, call a hotline. In cases of domestic abuse or child neglect, report it so that people can receive the help they need.

Animal liberation is a popular practice, and freeing animals that are to be killed saves lives. While this practice creates great merit, it is important to do it properly. Before buying animals to liberate, check that those animals are indeed in danger, and make sure the seller will not try to recapture them as soon as you release them, only to sell the animals again. If you release animals into bodies of water, ensure that they won't alter the natural ecological balance in that place. Release animals in a place where they will be safe, not where they are in danger of being hunted, trapped, or eaten by another animal.

It's always good to chant texts, prayers, or mantra out loud before liberating animals as that plants Dharma seeds in their mindstreams.

311

Giving Love

~

Giving love means giving encouragement, comfort, and emotional support. We can do that through counseling someone who asks for advice or encouraging someone when they suffer from self-doubt. Encouragement is especially important for children. Often just one adult showing genuine interest in a child who is starting to go down a wrong path is enough to turn that child's life around.

312

Giving the Dharma

~~~

Giving the Dharma is said to be the highest generosity. This is because teaching and sharing the Dharma empowers a person to create the causes of happiness and avoid the causes of suffering.

Teaching the Dharma is a great responsibility, because giving incorrect teachings can harm someone for many future lifetimes. For that reason, avoid setting yourself up as a Dharma teacher. There are many other ways to share the Dharma that are beneficial, for example, giving people Dharma books or telling them about temples and Dharma centers where excellent teachers explain the Dharma. Discussing Dharma methods to deal with emotional problems is a great way to aid friends and colleagues. Playing recordings of Dharma teachings or chanting out loud so animals can hear the sounds of mantra is also the generosity of the Dharma.

313

The Generosity of Receiving

Many people have difficulty receiving gifts because they feel undeserving or indebted to the giver or they think they are obliged to give a gift in return. When we rebuff the gift, we may believe that we are being humble, but our refusal to accept the gift may actually be motivated by a self-concern that seeks to avoid our own discomfort.

The person giving the gift has a virtuous and joyful mind. When we refuse their gift, we are denying them the opportunity to create merit from generosity and are spoiling the joy of their kind heart.

Learning to receive gifts graciously, without imputing all sorts of misconceptions on the simple act of giving and receiving, is itself an act of generosity.

314

The Buddha and Our Karma

~

Making a positive contribution to the world doesn't entail solving all the world's problems. Even the Buddha can't do that. Why not? The Buddha is omniscient—he knows all that exists—but he is not omnipotent; he doesn't have absolute control over all causes and conditions in the universe. If he were omnipotent, he would have already ended all suffering because there is no reason for the world's suffering to continue if there is a way to unilaterally stop it.

The Buddha has no hindrances to benefit sentient beings from his own side. However, his power is matched by the power of our karma. If our minds are closed and unreceptive, the Buddha's awakening influence cannot penetrate them. For example, the sun shines everywhere freely, but if a bowl is upside down, the sun cannot enter it. We must turn our minds upright through Dharma practice so the sunshine of the Buddha's awakening influence will enter them. This takes time and effort, but the resulting brilliance is spectacular.

315

Contributing with Joy

⁓

Although we lack the Buddha's awakening influence at present, we can still make a positive contribution to society and to those around us. Cultivate a compassionate motivation that is free from attachment, anger, and self-centeredness. Understand that you aren't the only conditioning factor in others' lives and cannot change their minds or control their environment. Then give whatever is appropriate: material goods, protection, love, or the Dharma, and take delight in doing so. Let go of expecting results or appreciation and simply rejoice in the act of giving with the motivation of kindness.

This attitude helps us remain more peaceful when we relate to people. It's also a more peaceful way to relate to ourselves, because we have a happy and positive motivation for whatever we do.

316

Maybe We're Not the One to Offer Help

As much as we may want to help, sometimes we are not the best person to offer help. For example, when a teenager challenges parental authority and the parents try to explain the disadvantages of risky behavior, the teen won't listen. But if another adult who is a trusted friend says the same words, the teen might heed the message.

If one member of a couple decides to leave the relationship, they are not the right person to console the other partner. That will only mislead the other partner with false hope that the relationship will resume. Instead, the other partner needs to rely on other friends to help them process the breakup.

317

Don't Confuse Attachment with Compassion

Attachment and compassion both draw us to another person with the wish for them to be happy and not suffer. The difference between them is that attachment is based on exaggerating the other person's good qualities, and it has a lot of strings attached. This form of affection is unstable and can turn into anger when expectations are not met. On the other hand, compassion is stable: it wants the other person to have happiness and freedom from suffering simply because they are a living being.

In the example in the previous entry, the person who left the relationship yet wants to comfort the partner has confused attachment with compassion. There is stickiness in the mind as well as a feeling of self-importance: *I am the one who can best comfort them.*

When we truly want the best for another person, we must sometimes step back and subdue our attachment and other afflictions.

318

What Are We Seeing and Touching?

In daily life, we say, "I see the cup," but what are we really seeing? We're actually seeing the color and shape of the cup. These are qualities of the cup—they are not the cup. But by seeing these qualities, we impute "cup" and think we see a cup existing objectively, "out there." Similarly, when touching the ceramic container that holds tea that is on the table, we say, "I touched the cup." But what did we actually touch? We touched the ceramic parts and felt their smoothness and coolness. These, too, are not the cup, but we impute "cup" based on these qualities and say we touched the cup.

It's interesting to investigate what we are actually seeing and touching and then observe that our mind imputes an object in dependence on those qualities or parts. Frequently reflecting like this helps us understand that things exist depending on factors that are not actually them (red is not a cup, smooth is not a cup), and for this reason these things are empty of existing from their own side.

319

Existing in Mutual Dependence

When we see a patch of the color blue, we have the feeling that a truly existent perceiving subject—the visual consciousness—is seeing a truly existent object, a patch of blue that exists objectively. We see the two as separate and distinct, independent of each other. It's as if the visual consciousness were always a visual consciousness, even if there are no external objects to be seen. Similarly, it seems as if the object exists out there, waiting to be seen.

In fact, the perceiving subject and the perceived object exist in relationship to each other. The visual consciousness is not a subject unless there are objects to be perceived. The patch of blue isn't an object unless there is the possibility of a subject perceiving it. The two exist in mutual dependence.

Be aware throughout the day of how all things are posited or designated in dependence on other things. They exist in relationship to each other, just as long and short, big and small exist in relation to each other. Such awareness is a good mindfulness practice to counteract our tendency to view everything as independent objects existing in and of themselves.

320

Justifying Anger

We often don't deal with our anger because we believe it's justified. *I don't need to apply an antidote. I need to put this person in their place.*

Sometimes we justify our anger as a protection because we fear others taking advantage of us. Here, small matters quickly become major ones, and with anger we feel empowered to stand up for ourselves. Other times we crave authority or respect and think that anger will bring that. But even if others bend and comply with our demands, internally they do not respect or like us.

We must debate with the reasons our angry attitude puts forth to justify itself. Remember, anger is a mental factor based on exaggerating or projecting harm that wants to harm whatever seems threatening. Just by its definition we know that anger is unrealistic.

321

Righteous Anger

In cases of injustice, we may believe that righteous anger is not only appropriate, but that it's the only motivation that could spur us to correct injustice in the world. But what about compassion? Can't it be a strong and even more effective motivation?

When anger clouds the mind, we do not think clearly, so the actions we undertake to stop the harm are not well thought out. Seeing the perpetrator of injustice as hateful, our minds become filled with hate, mirroring the very attitude we protest in the other. Like them, we too divide our world into "us versus them," helping those who agree with us and harming those who don't.

Compassion is concerned with the welfare of both the perpetrator and the victim. It seeks to understand the motivation and needs of both parties and to devise a solution that would meet the perpetrator's concerns without harming others. With compassion we express ourselves better, which facilitates communication.

To bring this perspective into current social situations, try to cultivate compassion for groups experiencing discrimination and those who discriminate against them. If we make an effort to understand how the latter group thinks, we may learn that their hatred and bias are based on fear. That gives us useful information needed to address their concerns. When their concerns are heard and met, their internal pressure to blame others for their unhappiness subsides.

322

Be Careful What You Get Jealous About

What would your life be like if you were that person you're jealous of? Imagine switching places with them and having all the qualities and opportunities they have. Would your life then be perfect?

We quickly see that whomever we're jealous of has their own set of problems. They have their own internal suffering, which sometimes derives from the very qualities and opportunities we're jealous of. Ask yourself, *Do I want to deal with all the disadvantages of their problems?*

As they say, be careful of what you're jealous of, because you might just get it. Then you'll have to deal with it.

323

Don't Press the "Send" Button

Sometimes we receive an email and have an intense urge to put the sender in his place. (If only we had so much enthusiasm for our Dharma practice!) We write a tart reply and press "send." Shortly afterward, we reflect, *Did I really write that?* We realize the other person will be unhappy to read what we sent; they will probably respond with hostility, and we'll have an even bigger problem than before.

What I've learned is not to respond to such messages, or at least not right away. Let them sit for a few hours or a day. Then, if we do respond, let our reply sit in the draft folder instead of immediately sending it. When our mind is calmer, review the email. If it has the appropriate tone and meaning, send it; otherwise press "delete."

324

Training in Wisdom and Compassion

With an ignorant mind, when we experience a pleasant ripening of karma, attachment swells up, motivating destructive karma for future unhappiness. When we experience an unpleasant ripening of karma, hostility rears up, motivating destructive actions that bring future misery.

The mind-training teachings known as *lojong* instruct us to train the mind to respond to whatever happens from a Dharma perspective—a mind that sees the experience as empty yet appearing, lacking its own inherent nature yet existing dependently. Mind training instructs us to see all events with eyes of compassion.

By training our mind to respond to all karmic ripenings in this way, we create the collections of merit and wisdom, the two fundamental causes of buddhahood. The attainment of buddhahood doesn't hinge on what happens to us, but on how we respond to it.

325

Democracy

We say we believe in democracy and that the popular vote wins.

On one side is *me*, and on the other is all sentient beings, minus one. Whose happiness is more important—mine or that of all-sentient-beings-minus-me? As believers in democracy, we would say that all-sentient-beings-minus-me is more numerous that just one person, *me*—that their happiness is of greater importance, and that the elimination of their suffering should matter more.

It's not all about *me*.

326

For the Dharma to Exist for a Long Time

Our own progress toward full awakening is not our only purpose in practicing; the preservation of the Dharma for future generations is essential. We have access to the precious teachings because millions of people practiced them over the centuries, keeping them alive as a living tradition to this very day. We come along—confused, full of afflictions and opinions—and can encounter the teachings and masters who embody them due to the kindness of those millions of people who have preceded us.

It is our job to practice purely and to maintain the transmitted scriptural Dharma as well as the realized, embodied Dharma, so that living beings who are confused and full of afflictions and opinions will have the possibility of meeting these teachings in the future.

And if we are fortunate, we may be among them.

327

Are We Ready to Go?

Most people who die on any given day didn't wake up in the morning and think, *I'm going to die today.*

News of another person's death is like a personal instruction from the Buddha to maintain our awareness of our mortality and evaluate our practice to see if we are prepared for death.

Are we satisfied with our Dharma practice?

Have we sufficiently purified our destructive karma and created merit?

Have we apologized to the people we need to apologize to and forgiven the people we need to forgive? If we can't do so directly, at least apologizing and forgiving in our mind is good.

Do we know how to guide our mind when we're dying? What practice will we do, and will we remember to practice when the process of dying begins?

Asking ourselves these questions gives us a lot of energy to practice in a pure way, without getting sidetracked by worldly concerns. If we can do this, dying will be a breeze.

328

A Guide to Making Good Decisions

In each choice there are short-term and long-term benefits and short-term and long-term disadvantages. From a Dharma perspective, the concerns of this life are considered short term, and preparing for future lives, liberation, and full awakening is considered long term. There are four permutations, and the Buddha gave advice for each:

If something is of short-term benefit and long-term benefit, do it.

If something is of short-term disadvantage and long-term disadvantage, don't do it.

The tricky ones are: what if it's of short-term benefit, but long-term disadvantage? Our intellect says, "Go for the long-term benefit." But when afflictions arise, we go for the short-term benefit and wind up with a long-term disadvantage.

If it's of short-term discomfort but long-term benefit, again, look to the long-term benefit.

329

The True Culprits

Nobody ever really wishes to harm others; they simply want to alleviate their own pain and are confused about how to do this. When someone harms you, don't burn with rage but instead see a suffering sentient being. If that person were happy, they wouldn't be doing the action that harms you. After all, no one wakes up in the morning and says, "The sun is shining and I feel wonderful. I think I'll go out and harm someone!"

People harm others when they are miserable. Although you may be used to viewing a harmer as a powerful, fearsome person, they are in fact a confused sentient being who doesn't realize they are creating the cause of their own misfortune by harming others. Instead of anger, have compassion for them and wish them to be free of suffering. Then not only will they be happy, they won't be acting in ways you find objectionable.

330

Doing Things We Don't Like to Do

Usually we avoid doing tasks that we don't like to do. We delegate the task to someone else, make an excuse, don't show up, or get distracted by something more important. Or we question the necessity of that activity or its timing, or why we are the only one who can do it.

On the other hand, we aspire to become bodhisattvas, beings whose hearts overflow with compassion and love for sentient beings and who work for their welfare without any hesitation or fear. We want to attain buddhahood, a state in which all obscurations have been eliminated and all excellent qualities brought to perfection.

Avoiding the tasks we find unpleasant severely limits actualizing our spiritual aims, doesn't it? There are no records of great bodhisattvas who said, "Sorry, I'll lead you to awakening but don't ask me to vacuum the floor."

331

I'm Too Busy

~

The one universal excuse that everyone uses these days and that no one dares to question is "I'm too busy." It often means "I don't want to do that," or maybe more honestly, "I'm too lazy to do that."

Why does "I'm too busy" always work? Because everyone is too busy. If you're not too busy, you don't have a life and something must be wrong with you. Even the things you do to relax make you too busy—you've got to go to the gym, you've got to read this book, you've got to take a nap.

Is our life really too busy, or is it our mind that is too busy?

332

The One Thing You Have to Do

⁓

We often say to ourselves, *I have to do this. I have to pick my kids up from school. I have to go to work early.* Actually, the only thing we ever have to do is die. Everything else is optional. Saying "I have to" indicates how little we see the freedom in our lives, how much we feel pressure and succumb to it. In fact, we have choice regarding many aspects of our lives.

If you choose not to pick your child up from school, there will be results that you don't want. Instead of complaining, say, *I'm choosing to pick my child up because I want her to be safe.* Then you do it with a happy mind and a good reason, instead of with resentment and obligation.

Saying "I'm *choosing* to do x-y-z" forces us to be honest about our choices instead of blaming our stress on others. Choice makes us responsible for our actions. In addition, choice opens up the possibility of enjoying what we do. As long as we're choosing to do an activity, let's make it fun for ourselves and everyone involved. Let's approach it with a smile instead of a frown.

333

The Opinion Factory

If you ever need an opinion, ask me. I have opinions about everything and everyone. It doesn't matter if they're accurate or not, my opinion factory continues to proliferate with opinions. Unfortunately, it doesn't face a layoff, a strike, or an electrical failure. It operates 24/7, filling my mind with nonsense and stress.

Our opinion factory starts when we're toddlers. "What do you want, orange juice or apple juice?" A toddler doesn't really care, but we make them care by asking this question. In kindergarten, a child is asked, "What's your favorite color?" Why is deciding on a favorite color important?

Wouldn't it be nice to shut down the opinion factory and just enjoy what's in front of us without always having to have an opinion about it?

334

The Anxiety Factory

⌢

When we enter a new situation, our anxiety factory steps up production. *What are these people doing? I like this, I don't like that. I don't understand this. What do they expect from me? Do I fit in? Do they like me? Do I like them? How can they benefit me? Will they take advantage of me?* We get tangled up in fear and insecurity.

Whenever such thoughts arise, try greeting them, *Oh yes, hello. I know you. You're here to disturb my inner peace*, and then let them go. Rather than let your mind proliferate with a variety of hopes and fears, come back to seeing the goodness that's before you in every person you encounter. Consider how you could bring some ease and friendliness into that person's life.

335

Not Enough Merit

~

A student once told me he was reluctant at the conclusion of his meditation sessions to dedicate his merit to sentient beings because he didn't have enough merit to afford to give any away.

I explained to him that he needn't fear, that our merit expands when we dedicate it for the welfare of all sentient beings. This is especially so when we dedicate for our own *and* others' awakening and for all the good circumstances conducive to this.

After hearing this, he happily chanted the verses to dedicate merit.

336

Chasing Our Tails

A friend gave my cats a toy mouse with a built-in laser pointer. The cats loved watching and chasing the red dot around, even though there was nothing to catch.

That's exactly how we are with sense pleasures. There's no real happiness in the object and nothing to hold onto, but our mind becomes captivated by whatever we think is beautiful, and we follow it everywhere. If it's a person, our eyes are glued to them; if it's a piece of fudge on the buffet table, we're watching to see who else might take it before we can get to it.

It's helpful to remember that all this is foolishness, that chasing after sense pleasures will only make us dizzy. Let's be human beings rather than copy the kitties that chase the uncatchable.

337

Taking Every Opportunity

An elderly woman who attended Dharma class told me that she and her husband of sixty-plus years always kissed each other on the check and said "I love you" whenever one of them left the house. Both of them were aware that their lifespans were uncertain, and in case something happened while one of them was away, they wanted the comfort of knowing that their last moment together was one of mutual appreciation and gratitude.

Even if we're comparatively young, the time we spend with another person may be the last time we're together. Let's make sure it is harmonious. If there is an unresolved disagreement when we part, let's at least acknowledge our underlying affection and respect for each other.

If we move through life solely focused on our own happiness, we'll grieve the large and small opportunities to connect with others when those opportunities are no longer there.

338

Mesmerized

Sports provide incredible opportunities for understanding the Buddha's teachings when you look at them in terms of people's motivations and their actions and results.

Many rich and famous athletes are confused by their fame and wealth, and some behave poorly, ruining their lives. They are experiencing the results of good karma but using those pleasurable results to create negative karma. Then you watch the audience. People get so excited about a ball. They're totally fixated by where this ball is and where they want it to go. Whether it's golf, baseball, soccer, or football, they are glued to the ball. But it's only a ball. It's the mind that makes the ball so important.

When we look at these people with human lives and intelligence—people who have the opportunity to end their cycle of rebirth but are mesmerized by a ball—we feel like crying.

339

What's Wrong with Pleasure?

Pleasure is not a problem. There's nothing evil about pleasure. The problem is our craving, clinging, and attachment to that pleasure.

Don't blame pleasure, but examine your experience and see what happens when you get attached to pleasure. Is your mind peaceful? Are you kindhearted? Do you treat others fairly? Or does your mind become narrow and obsessed with the person or object that gives you pleasure?

Spend some time thinking about how attachment hijacks your mind and causes you problems. What ideas do you have for how to subdue your attachment and its deleterious effects?

340

Our Most Precious Possession

~

Time is our most precious possession, and it's not in unlimited supply. Because of having time, we can create virtue and purify nonvirtue, learn the Dharma, and contribute to the well-being of others. Our possessions, dear ones, reputation, and popularity come and go, but how we choose to spend our time has long-lasting effects. We can waste our time or use it wisely. But no matter what we choose to do with our time, we cannot get it back. So let's be wise about how we spend our time and use it for what is valuable in the long run.

341

Shifting Perspectives

⌇

Relationships and events exist within multidimensional contexts. One element of that context is our subjective perspective; another is our mood.

One morning while our new monastic residence was being built, I heard the sound of banging and machines and thought, *We really need this new building. I'm happy that its construction is underway.*

But if we were in the midst of a meditation retreat and I heard the sound of saws buzzing and hammers pounding at our neighbors', I would complain, *This sound is disturbing our meditation. Why must they build something now?*

All this just goes to show that things are empty of true existence—nothing exists as pleasurable or painful from its own side.

342

Our Mind Is Like the Open Sky

The sky is pure, open space, free from all obstructions. The nature of our mind is similar: the afflictions, self-centered attitude, and other obscurations are not in its essential nature. Just as clouds may temporarily obscure the open sky, anger, attachment, and confusion can temporarily obscure our mind. When they do, the pure, open nature of the mind still remains; we just can't see it at the time.

By generating the wisdom realizing the emptiness of inherent existence, we will be able to eradicate obscurations from our mind forever and enjoy the sky-like spaciousness of a purified mind.

343

Pray to Have Problems

~

Mind-training texts instruct sincere practitioners to pray to have problems, because problems are fuel for generating bodhicitta.

Our problems are the result of our destructive karma, which was created under the influence of the self-centered attitude. So instead of responding with anger and creating more destructive karma, which only brings more problems, we give all of our suffering to the self-centered attitude and say, "You created the cause, now you experience the unhappy result."

It is important to remember that the self-centered attitude is not us; it is not who we are. It's an extra, corrupt attitude that can be eliminated. In that way, when we give the suffering to the self-centered attitude, our mind remains peaceful. In addition, we stop the continuum of creating destructive karma and instead destroy the real enemy, self-centeredness. As a result, our bodhicitta can grow.

344

Relaxing into Constant Change

At the beginning of each day it's helpful to reflect, *Everything that arises due to causes and conditions is transient. I'm changing moment by moment. My friends are transient. My problems don't even remain the same. Everything I have and everything I'm trying to achieve are also impermanent.* Thinking like this helps us to see that there's no use clinging to these things as fixed and then getting upset when they change.

That doesn't mean we don't have goals, forget about making plans, or that we stop caring about others. Rather, we see that getting aggravated and anxious about these things is unnecessary. It's like trying to stop a waterfall from flowing or the wind from blowing.

When things are in the nature of change, the only appropriate response is to relax and try to guide how they change with wisdom and compassion.

345

Seeds of Afflictions

~

To reduce and eliminate disturbing emotions and wrong views, we must know their causes. The stages of the path to awakening (*lamrim*) include six factors that cause afflictions to manifest in the mind: the seeds of afflictions, contact with certain objects, detrimental influences, exposure to the media, habits, and distorted attention.

One factor is having the predisposition or the "seeds" of afflictions. These are innate; as beings who haven't attained higher stages of the path, we are born with the seeds of afflictions. Having the seeds of afflictions means, for example, that we may not be angry right now, but the possibility of becoming angry in the future exists. We may be free from manifest anger in the morning, but when a circumstance at work is disagreeable, we get angry in the afternoon. Although our manifest anger fades with time, the seed remains on our mindstream. When we experience a situation that triggers it, anger manifests again. The seed of anger connects one instance of anger to the next.

As long we have the seeds of the various afflictions on our mindstream, we need to be very careful because any cooperative condition can provoke them and make them manifest.

346

Contact with Certain Objects

~

We're going along completely fine, but then someone praises us, and before we know it we're full of self-importance.

Contact with sweet, ego-pleasing words is an irresistable trigger that stimulates arrogance. For this reason, practitioners take precepts to avoid certain objects and situations that spark their afflictions. This is also the reason why we do retreat in a quiet place with few distractions—at home we have contact with so many people and objects that give rise to our afflictions.

Setting limits on what we expose ourselves to is not escaping from reality. For example, if we want to lose weight, we don't meet our friends at the ice cream parlor. If we want to stop drinking and drugging, we avoid parties where people are taking these substances. Avoiding contact with the people or things that spark strong attachment or animosity gives us the mental space to go deeper in our practice. This, in turn, enables us to cultivate the antidotes to our afflictions.

Once the afflictions are under control or have been completely eradicated, contact with these things and people don't trigger the arising of afflictions.

347

Detrimental Influences

The third cause of afflictions is detrimental influences such as bad friends. In a Buddhist context, a bad friend is somebody who incites our afflictions: they want to take us drinking, gambling, or out to watch a movie with a lot of sex and violence. They say, "Don't donate your money to a charity, keep it and we'll go on vacation."

Such people wish the best for us in a worldly way, but because they don't have the Dharma perspective on life, their idea of happiness doesn't take karma and future lives into account. They see us as their friend and want us to be happy right now. Unfortunately, such friendships take us away from the Dharma and may even lead us down the slippery slope of nonvirtuous actions.

We don't reject such people, but we don't make them our best friends either. Being careful about whom we associate with is wise since people can either trigger the seeds of our virtuous or nonvirtuous mental factors.

348

Exposure to the Media

—

Media includes various forms of communication, from literature to the internet, from the news to advertising to movies and everything in between. In our current society, the media has a tremendous influence on us. Advertising inculcates in us the idea that we are not good enough—we don't look like the models in the ads, we don't live in houses like those in films. The media spreads stereotypical images of how "real men" act and what women should be. It tells us that we need to use a certain brand of toothpaste to be a likable person. Teenagers look up to people in the media, sometimes even those involved in school shootings.

When we lack discriminating wisdom and don't realize how the media manipulates us, our psychological well-being is undermined and our afflictions easily manifest, leading to harmful actions. We need to be careful of the influence the media has on our lives and carefully decide how much we want to expose ourselves to it.

349

Habit

~

The fifth factor that causes afflictions to arise is habit. We have habitual emotional responses to specific types of events, many of which we learned growing up. We reenact particular behaviors in certain occasions. Someone criticizes us and we get angry and lash out. We go to a party and look for attractive people to go to bed with. Someone teases us and we withdraw in shame. Someone disagrees with our political views and we're incensed.

It's almost as if we live our lives on autopilot. While some of these emotional patterns and behaviors may have kept us safe as children, they no longer help us as adults. If anything, they become a form of self-sabotage that keeps us imprisoned in cyclic existence.

Let's use our introspective awareness to discern these patterns and our wisdom to dismantle them. In their place, let's train our body, speech, and mind in qualities we respect and behaviors that we want to enact. Doing so will bring us internal satisfaction, better relationships with others, and fresh insights on the path.

350

Distorted Attention

~

The sixth factor that causes afflictions to arise is distorted attention. This mental factor exaggerates good or bad qualities, or projects qualities that aren't there onto people, objects, and events. Based on distorted ways of thinking about these, afflictions easily control our mind.

For example, oblivious to this mechanism, we believe that what is foul is beautiful, that what is unsatisfactory in nature is real happiness, that what is impermanent will endure, and that what doesn't have its own nature has an inherent nature.

When an affliction arises either during meditation or in daily life, instead of following it, stop and investigate if you're seeing the object accurately. Initially, it may be hard to see our projections onto people and things, but gradually we will be able to discern them and then question their validity.

351

Intoxicants

~

Although not listed as one of the factors that stimulate afflictions, intoxicants certainly play a role in this. I've worked with incarcerated people for two decades and would say that 99.9 percent of them were high on intoxicants when they engaged in the action that landed them in prison with a lengthy sentence. Similarly, most date rapes on college campuses occur when intoxicants are involved. And we all know of the many car accidents that happen due to drunk driving.

This doesn't mean that intoxication causes unwise actions, but it sure facilitates them. Many people think, *I can control myself even when I'm intoxicated. I wouldn't do anything stupid.* Does arrogance lie behind that self-assuredness?

A mother told me that her husband proudly collected liquor bottles, and her son followed his example in liking liquor. But one evening the son was driving under the influence and smashed into a car, killing four people. The son wound up in the ICU on several machines to keep him alive, until the prognosis dimmed and his parents decided to pull the plug. I couldn't imagine what a painful decision that was for the parents. The father went home and smashed his entire collection of liquor bottles.

352

Moving toward Our Spiritual Goals

We can't progress on the path by just knowing what we don't want to do or be. We should also know very clearly what we do want to go toward. This entails knowing the excellent qualities of the Buddha, the Dharma, and the Sangha and our potential to become them. We must have some idea what true paths, true cessations, and nirvana are, as well as the advantages of attaining these. Why should we understand the emptiness of inherent existence? What is the purpose of generating bodhicitta? How does renouncing cyclic existence and aspiring for freedom benefit me?

Having clear spiritual goals keeps us on track. We become open to following the instructions of reliable spiritual mentors and are willing to put energy into actualizing the aims we seek because we are sure that they are worthwhile and valuable.

353

Passing Time

At the beginning of our lives we pass our time as children playing, checking up on our friends on Facebook, and trying to get into good schools. This goes on for a good twenty-five years (it used to be eighteen). It doesn't really end when we're twenty-five either.

In the second period of our lives, many people settle down—get a job, get married, have kids, work to support the family. We also do everything we need to do to be successful in our careers, because it's not just family that's important, we also need status. We spend a good period of our life doing just that.

Finally, when it's time to retire—and sometimes we don't retire—we spend our time playing golf, visiting the grandchildren, and trying to decipher our Medicare bills.

Then death comes, and we're totally unprepared.

Let's transform our minds and tap into our Buddha potential now, while we still have the chance.

354

Transforming Our Mind

~

There's a Tibetan story about a man who diligently circumambulated a stupa while reciting mantra. Observing him, Lama Atisha said, "It's good that you're circumambulating the stupa, but it'd be better if you practiced the Dharma." So the man started doing lots of prostrations. Lama Atisha told him it's good he's prostrating, but it'd be better if he practiced the Dharma. Then the man started chanting scriptures, but Atisha told him the same thing. Puzzled, the man asked, "What is the meaning of 'practicing the Dharma'?" to which Atisha replied, "Transforming your mind into virtue."

Do we dress in Tibetan garb, ring bells, play ritual drums, and wear a mala around our neck, thinking we're practicing the Dharma? If so, Lama Atisha may have some wise advice for us.

355

Having a Kind Heart

~

With a kind heart, we don't want to harm others. Ethical conduct flows naturally.

With a kind heart, we don't want to harm ourselves, and we disengage from self-sabotaging activities.

With a kind heart, we want to benefit others and engage in actions that create positive energy and merit.

We've never heard of a Buddha who lacked a kind heart.

356

The Measure of Our Practice

~

How do we know we're making progress? Here are some considerations:

Do we get as angry as before? When we are angry, can we subdue the anger by applying the antidotes? Or do we suppress our anger and pretend we don't have it?

Can we acknowledge our ethical transgressions without concealing them or shaming ourselves, and make amends?

When we're in pain or receive bad news, does our mind turn to the Three Jewels? Do we remember the Dharma we've learned?

When we encounter others who are unhappy or experiencing suffering, does the wish to help them arise, or do we think of ways to leave the situation quickly?

Do we take delight when hearing others receive praise, or is there a twang in our heart wishing it were us?

Are we more honest about our faults and weaknesses? Do we give ourselves credit for our good qualities without being arrogant?

357

Choosing a Spiritual Mentor

~

Since we need a teacher to learn to drive and type, surely we also need one to transform our mind, which is a much more delicate process. We must examine a person's qualities carefully before deciding to establish a mentor-student relationship with them. Choosing someone to become one of our spiritual mentors is more important than deciding whom to marry, because our choice of spiritual mentors influences many lifetimes to come.

According to the scriptures, a qualified spiritual mentor should keep good ethical conduct, have meditation experience, and have a correct understanding of the ultimate truth. They must be compassionate, patient, and have a pure motivation for teaching (not seeking status, reputation, and offerings). While that person may have a good sense of humor and an enchanting personality, it is important to note that charisma is not listed as a characteristic of a qualified spiritual mentor.

358

Creating Identities

~

We build up many identities about ourselves: I am this race, I am this nationality, I am this ethnicity, I am this religion, I am this gender, I am this sexual orientation, I have this temperament. We learn and create so many identities in this life and impute significance to each of them. We have identities based on our occupation—I am a factory worker, a doctor, a monastic, a teacher, a musician, a clerk, a student, a hacker (oops, shouldn't tell people that). We create identities around our hobbies—I collect antiques, I coach soccer, I am a rock climber, I am a surfer, I love cooking, I like to go jogging.

We associate the self with these identities and give meaning to these labels. We think of ourselves in a certain way and have ideas about how people should treat us based on our various identities. We often think in terms of "us" and "them" and accuse others of not understanding our identities. We become offended when people don't treat us according to our identities. When we first meet someone, we tell them our identities so that they will know who we are.

However, on closer examination, we discover that we are not these identities. They are merely ideas manufactured by our minds and are based on many other factors. And none of these identities come with us to the next life.

359

Water Off a Duck's Back

~

Once day while I was working with Lama Thubten Yeshe on a project, many people came to see him, either to ask a question about what to do or to complain about what someone else did or to criticize what someone wanted to do. Lama was present with each person and responded compassionately, with full attention to each and every issue, and when the person left he returned to the project. There was no lingering mood from the previous interaction, no "Whew, I'm glad that person left" or "What a jerk! Why can't he work it out himself?" or "You'd think that person was a child with the way they're making a big deal out of nothing." It was like water off a duck's back. He just listened, dealt with what was important, and let go of everything else (unlike me, who had judgments and opinions about each person).

Lama lived in the moment, with awareness of the past and future, but he didn't cling to any of it and didn't waste his time proliferating with opinions about anything.

360

A World with No Buddha

What would happen if we lived in a world where the Buddha had not appeared and there were no teachings? What would it be like to live in a place with no Sangha community, scriptures, or spiritual mentors? Imagine living somewhere without religious freedom, where you could be arrested and imprisoned simply for chanting prayers or meditating? We could otherwise have many wonderful conditions for a good life, but we wouldn't be able to meet a path that nourished our spiritual needs despite our spiritual longing. The path to awakening would be totally blocked.

What would happen if we were born as a person who had no spiritual interest at all? What if the goals of our life were only to make money, become famous, receive praise from people we value, and have a good sex life?

Spend some time imagining being in those situations. Then come back to your present situation. You have fortune that is beyond amazing. Please make good use of it to transform your mind.

361

Whatever Comes Together Separates

~

Whatever comes together must also separate; there's no way around it.

I led a most remarkable memorial service for a man in his thirties who died of cancer. He and his wife were high-school sweethearts and had been married for over ten years. At the service she stood up, and with eyes glowing with love and a voice filled with passion, said to her deceased husband, "We shared so much love together, and I am full of love. Now that you are gone, I will share all that love with others!"

To her, love did not come in a fixed quantity. The more she had, the more she shared, and she shared her love broadly.

362

No Matter How Long It Takes

We've had afflictions in our minds since beginningless time, and we're well-habituated with them so it's going to take awhile to cleanse our mind. As such, we need to develop a long-term perspective that's willing to apply consistent effort to create the causes for happiness and to remove the causes of suffering.

Fortitude in practicing the path helps us to endure difficulties, and joyous effort brings delight in creating virtue. To maintain joyous effort, contemplate the benefits of attaining awakening and the disadvantages of remaining in cyclic existence. As the benefits become clear, we'll see that it's the only way to go and will naturally put energy into it. It doesn't matter how long it takes because we know we're doing something valuable for ourselves and others in the long run.

363

Reflect for a Minute

~

Reflect for a minute on the kindness of others—the kindness not only of friends and family, but also of strangers whose work in society helps us. Reflect on the benefit you receive from people who challenge you: they help you to discover resources within yourself that you didn't know you had.

Seeing how dependent you are on others to stay alive and how much benefit you've received from them, respond from your heart with a wish to repay that kindness. Wish to make a positive contribution to the welfare of other living beings.

Your spiritual practice is one way to make a positive impact, because by progressing along the path, your capability to be of direct benefit to others and to work for their welfare increases by leaps and bounds.

364

Crying and Laughing

~

Before we know how to drive, learning the skills of navigating a car, merging on the highway, and learning all the rules of the road appear to be arduous. But after we learn these skills, we wonder why we were so intimidated and thought it was so difficult.

Every day the Indian sage Lama Atisha saw a woman who alternately cried and laughed. Perplexed, he asked if she was mentally distressed. She replied, "No. I cry because sentient beings are bound in suffering. They have the buddha-nature, yet unable to see that, they suffer. I laugh because when they know the nature of their minds, the small difference between ignorance and wisdom is cleared and they can easily be liberated."

While we are in the midst of cyclic existence, the difference between ignorance, which is the root of our misery, and wisdom, which is the key to awakening, seems enormous. We must exert much effort to purify our minds and cultivate excellent qualities. Yet after we attain awakening, the obstacles seem so small. It was just a matter of perspective.

365

Think Big

~

Think big about how we can help the Dharma to exist on our planet for many generations to come. Think of all the sentient beings who will benefit from that as the ripple effect goes out. When we contribute to sustaining the Dharma in this world, we'll reap the benefits in our future lives in practical ways. If we're born on this earth in the future, we'll be able to take advantage of the monasteries, Dharma centers, websites, books, and so forth that we helped to create in our previous lives. We'll also benefit karmically by acting with bodhicitta, which will lead to our full awakening.

FURTHER READING

Chodron, Thubten. *Don't Believe Everything You Think: Living with Wisdom and Compassion*. Boston: Snow Lion Publications, 2012.

————. *Open Heart, Clear Mind: An Introduction to the Buddha's Teachings*. Ithaca, NY: Snow Lion Publications, 1990.

————. *Working with Anger*. Ithaca, NY: Snow Lion Publications, 2001.

Dhammananda, K. Sri. *How to Live without Fear and Worry*. Kuala Lumpur: Buddhist Missionary Society, 1989.

Dilgo Khyentse Rinpoche. *Enlightened Courage: An Explanation of the Seven-Point Mind Training*. Ithaca, NY: Snow Lion Publications, 2006.

First Dalai Lama, Gyalwa Gendum Druppa. *Training the Mind in the Great Way*. Translated by Glenn H. Mullin. Ithaca, NY: Snow Lion Publications, 1997.

H.H. Tenzin Gyatso, the Fourteenth Dalai Lama. *Cultivating a Daily Meditation*. Dharamsala, India: Library of Tibetan Works and Archives, 1991.

————. *Ethics for the New Millennium*. New York: Riverhead Books, 2001.

————. *Healing Anger: The Power of Patience from a Buddhist Perspective*. Ithaca, NY: Snow Lion Publications, 1997.

Hopkins, Jeffrey. *Cultivating Compassion: A Buddhist Perspective.* New York: Broadway Books, 2001.

———. *A Truthful Heart: Buddhist Practices for Connecting with Others.* Ithaca, NY: Snow Lion Publications, 2008.

Jinpa, Thupten, translator. *Mind Training: The Great Collection.* Boston: Wisdom Publications, 2006.

Khandro Rinpoche. *This Precious Life: Tibetan Buddhist Teachings on the Path to Enlightenment.* Boston: Shambhala, 2005.

Kolts, Russell, and Thubten Chodron. *An Open-Hearted Life: Transformative Methods for Compassionate Living from a Clinical Psychologist and a Buddhist Nun.* Boston: Shambhala, 2013.

McDonald, Kathleen. *How to Meditate: A Practical Guide*, rev. ed. Boston: Wisdom Publications, 2005.

Rabten, Geshe, and Geshe Ngawang Dhargyey. *Advice from a Spiritual Friend*, rev. ed. Boston: Wisdom Publications, 2001.

Rinchen, Geshe Sonam. *The Thirty-Seven Practices of Bodhisattvas: An Oral Teaching.* Ithaca, NY: Snow Lion Publications, 1997.

Shantideva and the Padmakara Translation Group. *The Way of the Bodhisattva.* Boston: Shambhala, 2006.

Tegchok, Geshe Jampa. *The Kindness of Others: A Commentary on the Seven-Point Mind Training.* Weston, MA: Lama Yeshe Wisdom Archives, 2006.

———. *Transforming Adversity into Joy and Courage: An Explanation of the Thirty-seven Practices of Bodhisattvas.* Ithaca, NY: Snow Lion Publications, 2005.

Thubten Zopa Rinpoche, Lama. *The Door to Satisfaction: The Heart Advice of a Tibetan Buddhist Master*. Boston: Wisdom Publications, 1994.

———. *Kadampa Teachings*. Boston: Lama Yeshe Wisdom Archive, 2010.

———. *Transforming Problems into Happiness*. Boston: Wisdom Publications, 2001.

Tsering, Geshe Tashi. *The Awakening Mind: The Foundation of Buddhist Thought*. Boston: Wisdom Publications, 2008.

ABOUT THE AUTHOR

Bhikshuni Thubten Chodron is an American Buddhist nun in the Tibetan tradition. Ordained in 1977, she is a student of H.H. the Dalai Lama and other Tibetan masters. She teaches Buddhism internationally, is the author of many Dharma books, including *Buddhism for Beginners*, and is the founder and abbess of Sravasti Abbey, a Buddhist monastic community in Washington State, USA, where she lives. See www.thubtenchodron.org and www.sravasti.org.